THE JOY OF FISHING

. . . can be yours no matter how young you are or how little money you have to spend.

This book will teach you how to make your own simple tackle, at practically no cost—how to raise or find your own bait—how to make your own lures—what to fish for in the local pond, river or stream—how and where to catch fish, and even how to cook them!

There's no need to wait to learn the joy of fishing. Learn now—and enjoy it all the rest of your life.

Books by Joseph D. Bates, Jr.

Spinning for American Game Fish
Trout Waters and How to Fish Them
Streamer Fly Fishing in Fresh and Salt
    Water
Spinning for Fresh Water Game Fish
Spinning for Salt Water Game Fish
The Outdoor Cook's Bible
Streamer Fly Tying & Fishing
    (with a subscribed limited edition
    of 600 copies)
Elementary Fishing

ELEMENTARY FISHING

JOSEPH D. BATES, JR.

Illustrated by
LARRY BRADLEY LANE

Front Cover Illustration by
MILTON C. WEILER

POPULAR LIBRARY • NEW YORK

CONTENTS

What Departments of Natural Resources Do—Value of
Wardens and Game Protectors—"If You Would Catch
More, You Must Kill Less"—What the Money from Fish-
ing Licenses Does—Why Fish Laws Are Necessary—Fire
Prevention.

INTRODUCTION

Somebody who works for the government has figured out that about ten percent of fishermen catch about ninety percent of the fish! If you are part of the "unlucky" majority—or if you have never enjoyed fishing before, but would like to know how—it merely is necessary to learn a few simple facts to put you among the "lucky" ones.

Actually, luck has very little to do with success in fishing. It's knowledge and skill that count. This book will provide the essential knowledge. Skill comes with practice, but it takes very little skill to have a great deal of fun and good luck in fishing!

If you have no tackle, that's no problem. In this book we learn how to start fishing with merely a hook and a few feet of monofilament line costing only a few pennies at the most. The rod (or I guess we should call it a fishing pole, in this case) can be cut from a bush or sapling beside the lake or stream. Many kinds of bait are free for the finding, and we learn here how to find them, how to rig them, and how and where to fish with them.

This is all that is needed to start with—and you'll be surprised at the number and variety of fish you can catch with this simple tackle.

Then we learn how to graduate to better equipment and how to choose between the various methods of fly fishing, spinning, spin casting and plug casting. After this we learn how to cast with the tackle, where and how to fish with it, and what kinds of baits or lures work best for what kinds of fish under various conditions. This tackle need cost very little, and can be acquired gradually. To keep the investment as low as possible, this book tells how to make your own lures, leaders, flies and other essentials. These pleasant projects not only save money, but also provide interesting things to do on winter evenings or during rainy days at camp.

We hope this book will explain why fishing should be for fun, rather than a competition to see how many we can catch. We hope it will explain why the greatest fun is in using light tackle, for added thrills and to give the fish a fair chance. (Too many people miss most of the fun of fishing by using gear that is too strong just so they quickly can "haul them in.") We also hope this book will explain why sport fish should not be wasted; why the little ones usually should be released to grow up, and why there is great satisfaction even in releasing some of the big ones so someone else can enjoy fishing for them on another day.

But of course we want to keep a few, and know how to clean them properly, keep them fresh and cook them deliciously—even outdoors with little or no equipment. So this book ends with recipes and suggestions for cleaning and preserving fish—and we hope it will help many beginners to enjoy countless fun-filled days of successful fishing!

More books have been written about angling than about any other sport. But, surprisingly enough, there seems to be no book which outlines the simple, basic facts of how to start fishing easily and sensibly without having to buy expensive tackle. Talks with Scout executives, Izaak Walton League leaders and others who like to help people enjoy the outdoors indicated that such a book is badly needed. But to publish one at a price anyone can afford seemed almost impossible.

One day I sat in the comfortable office of Mrs. Madeline McGill, at the Wright & McGill Company in Denver, Colorado. Her company makes the famous Eagle Claw brand of fishhooks, rods and other fishing equipment, but Mrs. McGill is primarily interested in helping young people enjoy the fun of fishing. So we discussed the problem.

"You write the book and have it published," she said. "We'll pay for it and distribute it on a nonprofit basis to everyone who wants it."

So the friendly people of Wright & McGill are doing their good turn for thousands of people, both young and older, who want to start to enjoy fishing economically and sensibly —and perhaps also for many youth-group leaders who need a book outlining a simple method of fishing instruction. If this book is pleasing to all concerned, I shall be very grateful.

JOSEPH D. BATES, JR.

Longmeadow, Massachusetts

CHAPTER I

STARTING IN—WITH
NEXT TO NOTHING

Many years ago my dog and I used to travel across the Western Massachusetts fields down to the brook, and sometimes as far as the river. Muskrats had their homes in its banks and backwaters, and we would sit and watch them repairing their houses or swimming about in search of food. Ducks flew in occasionally, and I learned to identify the various kinds. Songbirds and flowers were everywhere. Both the brook and the river were so clean that we could drink from them and swim in them. I wish it was that way there today.

When we walked up to a pool in the brook, several trout would scoot for cover. So we learned to crawl up to the pools quietly. When we did so the trout were unafraid, because they didn't know we were there. We could see them at the edge of the shadows cast by the trees and bushes into the pools, or before or behind a log or rock. There they rested placidly, with fins and tail scarcely moving unless they decided to dash out occasionally to swirl to the surface to pick up an insect or a nymph or some other kind of food.

The brook also contained small bass and chubs and other fish that probably swam in from the river. Schools of minnows darted here and there, their silvery bodies shining in the sun as they twisted through the underwater plants and among the pebbles to find tiny things to eat. The brook was sparkling clear, and was full of fish and of food for them. So I would lie with my face parting the grasses along the brook and spend hours watching what went on there.

My dog, of course, didn't share this interest. So he would sleep nearby in the field in the sun. Occasionally he became tired of this and would jump into the pool. This disturbed the fish, so I would get up and go somewhere else. But when I returned, half an hour or so later on, the fish again were in their accustomed places and the pool was as quiet and peaceful as before.

I was only ten or twelve years old at the time and, as I remember it, had just joined the Boy Scouts. My allowance was only a few pennies a week, but one day I spent most of it to buy a few small fishhooks and a little spool of fishing line. This investment—probably the best one I ever made—started a lifetime love of fishing. Now, many years later, I have an abundance of fine tackle and have caught big fish in many parts of the world—but I don't think I ever had as much fun anywhere as I did during those early days along the brook near home.

So, with the hooks and the fishing line, my dog and I went back to the brook again. On the way I cut a limber green willow branch from a tall bush, trimmed off the leaves, and cut the tip back to a place where it seemed strong enough. At the end of this six-foot fishpole I tied on about six feet of the line, with a hook on the end. After turning over a few rocks in the field, I found a worm and put it on the hook. Then I crawled to the pool—very quietly, so not to disturb the fish.

A fairly big trout was placidly resting near a rock, a foot or two deep in the pool. I had seen him there many times before and knew that, no matter where he went, he always returned to this spot. It was his spot, and I often had seen him drive other fish away from it.

Since I had learned that any unusual motion on my

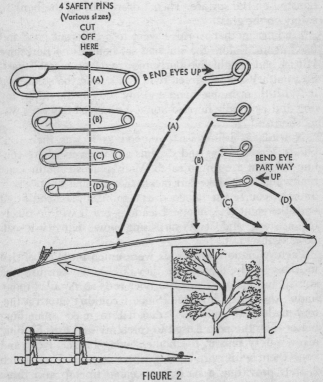

FIGURE 2
IDEAS FOR HOMEMADE FISHPOLES

part would drive him away, I decided not to drop the worm close to him. By raising the willow fishpole up and briskly forward, I made the worm drop into the pool several feet upstream from where he was, and he remained undisturbed. The worm sank down in the current and drifted toward the trout.

When the trout noticed the worm he dashed out and took it. On the end of the short line he raced around the pool, bending the willow pole until I thought it might break. But the tackle held and the trout thrashed on the surface, gradually becoming tired. It was so much fun to watch him, with his brilliant spots and colorful sides shining in the sun, that I let him fight until he lay exhausted on the surface. Then I drew him up the bank to safety on the grass.

Finding another worm, I went to a different pool and tried again. Before the sun had set behind the Berkshire Hills I had caught five fairly big trout and a small bass. So I cut a V-shaped green twig and strung the six fish on it. With them in one hand and my pole in the other, my dog and I proudly hurried home. From that day on I was a fisherman!

Nowadays, fishing isn't as good as it was then. But ponds, brooks, lakes and streams almost everywhere contain fish that are fun to catch. Many places contain some real whoppers! Makeshift tackle like my first willow pole outfit of course isn't as good as a tubular glass rod fitted with the right reel, line and leader—but it will do nicely for a start, and it is surprising how many fish can be caught with it.

Factory-made fishing rods were much more expensive in those early days than they are now, because the sturdy and economical glass fiber rods so popular today hadn't then been invented. Since I couldn't afford a factory-made rod anyway, I decided to make something better than the pole I used to catch my first fish. Finding a few safety pins in the home sewing basket, I cut and bent them with wire-cutting pliers as shown in sketch 2, thus providing a fairly serviceable tip top and three line guides for my new pole.

The reel was a problem, but a Y-shaped forked branch cut from a sapling worked fairly well. As the sketch shows, I trimmed off all but two of the outward extending side branches and left these two about five inches long. The lower trunk was cut to the same size, and the part away from the two side branches was shaved with a jackknife to fit the pole. This was lashed on with electrician's tape to provide a comfortable rod grip as well as a reel. Tip top and line guides were wound in place with heavy sewing thread, which then was varnished so that these were similar to windings on rods which cost money. The line was tied under this makeshift

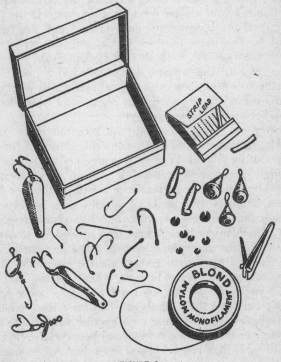

FIGURE 3
A BASIC TACKLE KIT

reel and was wound around it, then passed through the line guides and the tip top.

With this arrangement I could let out as much line as desired. If I hooked a big fish which wanted to run, I could let him take line off the reel by turning the rod grip from side to side. Also, I could control the line with the pressure of my thumb. Regained line had to be wound back on by hand, of course.

Another idea for a reel was two clamp-type clothespins, clamped to the grip, as shown. This worked fairly well, but wasn't as good as the forked branch because the clamps sometimes slipped, and it wasn't as easy to control the line. These two ideas, however, led to many others which I'll let readers have the fun of discovering for themselves. I always went to Scout camps in the summer, and we spent rainy days finding out who could think up and make the best tackle, and then who could catch the best fish with it. Our leaders made sort of a game of this; the winner always received a prize. This usually was a big box of marshmallows which we would share around the campfire that night—and which would have been issued to us anyway!

Later on, when there was no room to carry much tackle, for instance when I was in the islands of the Pacific during World War II, I learned always to carry enough essentials to catch fish. A coin purse or small metal or plastic box of similar size will do the job. In it are a dozen or two hooks of various sizes and a small spool containing not over fifty yards of about six-pound test monofilament line. A few strips of lead for sinkers, a small wobbler and spinner or two, and a few small bucktail flies are more than enough for the essentials. These vary, of course, depending on where we are and the kinds and sizes of fish we want to catch. Loose hooks won't tangle if their bends are laid on a few inches of transparent adhesive tape with another strip of the tape stuck over them. Thus sandwiched between the two layers of tape, they can be pulled out or torn off as needed. Another way is to string them through the eyes with a safety pin.

You'll think of a few other small tackle items which could be included, such as a fingernail nipper for cutting monofilament, but these are individual choices. The important thing is to make up this small and very inexpensive kit and to carry it always on outdoor excursions. Soldiers, hikers and explorers consider it an important element in their survival kits, but it's always handy for elementary fishing for everybody.

As I grew older, and advanced in Scouting, I began to read books and magazine articles about fishing. I learned how important it is to sneak up on fish without being seen, and that walking heavily along a stream bank can send echoes into the water which will alarm fish and prevent them from taking any lure whatsoever. Books show that, due to the refraction (or bending) of light rays entering the water, fish sometimes can see fishermen when

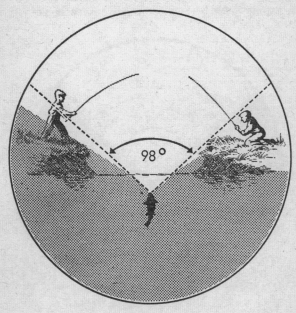

FIGURE 4
OVERHEAD CONE OF VISION OF A FISH

fishermen can't see fish. So keeping out of sight is all the more important because of this.

But in some cases fishermen can see fish when the fish can't see them. This is because fish have cone-shaped vision. Ahead, they can see whatever is in the cone area, and they also can see to the sides. But they can't see what is going on behind them. Thus, regardless of what tackle we're using, if we want to sneak up on fish so they can't see us in front of them or from the side, the answer is to approach them from behind. So since fish in moving water nearly always face upstream in the current, a good trick is to approach them from the downstream side.

In rigging these essentials of tackle we should learn two knots for tying the monofilament line to the hook. Just any old knot won't do. Since the knot usually is the weakest place in the line or leader, it is important to use the strongest and most suitable one we know.

In fishing with bait, we'll usually use a hook with a

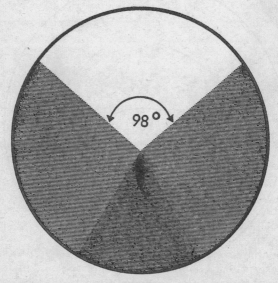

FIGURE 5
FORWARD CONE OF VISION OF A FISH

ringed (straight) eye; that is, with an eye which is neither bent up nor bent down. For such a hook most fishermen prefer the Clinch knot, or the Improved Clinch knot, and they think that the Improved Clinch knot is the more secure of the two, especially when the monofilament or leader material being used is very fine in diameter. Here are drawings of both ways to tie this knot:

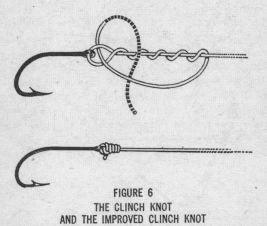

FIGURE 6
THE CLINCH KNOT
AND THE IMPROVED CLINCH KNOT

The two versions are very easy to tie and should be learned before going fishing. To tie the Clinch knot we merely thread several inches of the monofilament through the eye of the hook and then wind the end back around the monofilament above the hook five or six times in a spiral, as shown. The end of the monofilament then is slipped through the loop thus made above the hook's eye. By holding the hook and monofilament end in one hand and the upper part of the line in the other, we can pull the spiral coils tightly against the eye of the hook, thus making a secure and neat knot. The excess is clipped off closely.

The Improved Clinch knot is tied exactly the same way except that before pulling it tight the end, in addition to the above, also is slipped through the side loop, as the drawing shows. (With very small hooks and very fine monofilament—4 or 5X—this knot is even stronger when the monofilament end is passed through the hook eye *twice* before tying the knot.) All knots should be pulled tight slowly so they will gather properly.

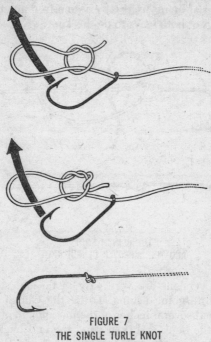

FIGURE 7
THE SINGLE TURLE KNOT
AND THE DOUBLE TURLE KNOT

In fishing with hooks with eyes not straight, but turned either up or down, it is preferable to use the Double Turle knot because it comes out straight through the eyes of this kind of hooks. This easy knot is made by threading the monofilament through the eye of the hook and then sliding the hook back up the line or leader, out of the way. The end of the monofilament then is doubled back on itself and a slipknot is made with the free end around the upper part. If two turns (as shown) are made in the slipknot instead of one, this will be a Double Turle knot. (One turn, or a simple slipknot, makes it a Single Turle knot.) When this slipknot is pulled tight, the result is a running slipknot, or "noose." Now let the hook slide back down the line to this loop and pass the loop over the rear of the hook so the line can pull it tight around the shank just behind the eye of the hook. The drawing shows this clearly, and it is easier to do than to describe. This knot is used with all hooks having turned up or turned down eyes, which includes the great majority of artificial flies.

Even new monofilament will kink into coils, which makes it difficult to cast. It will become especially kinky if wound around a homemade reel such as has been described and left that way for a long time. There is a simple remedy for this. Let out all the line you think you'll

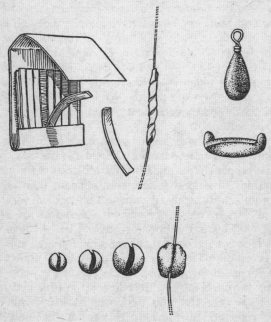

FIGURE 8
STRIP LEADS, SINKERS AND SPLIT SHOT

use, and hook the hook solidly into a tree or stump. By walking backward to the end of the line, you can pull the line as strongly as necessary to remove the kinks and thus make it limp again. This straightens the line and makes it supple and easy to cast. It also tests it for weak spots.

When using simple baits such as the worms and other kinds we will learn about in the next chapter, we may need a little lead to get them down in deep holes or fast currents where the big fish often lie. Drawing 8 shows common split shot, sinkers and strip lead (which often comes in folders like matchbooks). Lead usually should be applied on line or leader a foot or more above the hook, so the baited hook can move more freely in the current. Strip lead is wound spirally around the line or leader until it is a compact cylinder. This is easy to remove and to adjust. It catches between underwater stones and branches less often than split shot and other forms of sinkers. Split shot must be pinched onto the line or leader with small pliers or something similar. If not pinched on too tightly, it can be adjusted up or down on the line. If pinched on too tightly it is difficult to remove and may weaken the line. No lead should be added to the tackle unless necessary. When necessary, the less used the better.

In Chapter III we'll see why the hook is the most important part of simple tackle, and we'll learn how to select the proper shapes and sizes for all kinds of fishing. In bait fishing, one kind is far more efficient than all the others and, fortunately, it can be obtained at very low cost at tackle stores everywhere in almost all styles and sizes. This is the popular Eagle Claw—a hook design which is so efficient that over a million are made and sold every day. This is because, as sketch 9 shows, the point is curved inward toward the eye of the hook, thus putting the barb in the direct line of pull for maximum *hooking power*. Also, this design of hook is offset both to the right and to the left. This results not only in a balanced hook, but also in one which twists into the jaws of a fish to provide much greater *holding power*. Fisher-

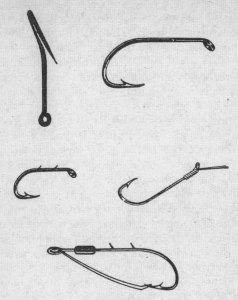

FIGURE 9

(TOP) FRONT AND SIDE VIEWS OF AN "EAGLE CLAW" HOOK (MIDDLE) A BAIT-
HOLDER HOOK AND A SNELLED HOOK (BOTTOM) A WEEDLESS BAITHOLDER
HOOK

men know that many hooks pull out, and they often get
strikes without hooking the fish at all. This happens sometimes with ordinary hooks; it happens very rarely with
the Eagle Claw design.

Hooks are so important in fishing that we'll discuss
them frequently in this book in the hope that, after the
book has been read, the reader will know exactly what
size and shape to select for every kind of fishing. In bait
fishing, one shape may be better for use with one kind of
bait, another for another kind. Proper selection means
better fishing. Basically, however, if in doubt about two
sizes, select the smaller one so the fish can see the hook
less easily. If in doubt about selecting a long-shank hook
or a short-shank hook, select the shortest one which will
do the job properly.

In the last drawing we have illustrated the qualities just mentioned about the famous Eagle Claw design. Here also is the same hook with "baitholder" features of two barbs on the shank. This feature holds bait such as live worms, grubs and plastic worms up on the shank of the hook rather than letting the bait slide down around the hook's bend, where it won't catch as many fish.

The drawing also shows an Eagle Claw weedless hook whose nylon bonded weed guard is much more effective than ordinary types because the nylon bonding helps prevent the guard from breaking off and allows it to be adjustable for proper tension. This is used with many kinds of baits when fishing in weedy or brushy places, but should be used only when necessary to prevent the hook from snagging or catching weeds. Weedless hooks are available both in regular and in baitholder types. Finally, the drawing shows a snelled hook, available in all suitable types and sizes for bait fishing.

This chapter has tried to show that anyone can begin to enjoy fishing with little or nothing in the way of tackle. For example, a group of a dozen or so young people can club together to invest only a dollar or so (for the whole group!) to buy a package or two of hooks and a spool of monofilament. By sharing these, they can have the fun of starting to enjoy fishing as the author did so many years ago. As a Scouter and former Scout, I suggest that this is something Scout leaders of both sexes should consider. There are perch, crappies, bluegills and other pond fish free for the taking merely by dropping a baited hook in the water from a boat, from a dock or from the shore. There are trout, bass and other tackle busters in lakes, brooks and streams everywhere which can be caught with this elementary tackle, thus starting beginners on a lifetime of fun in fishing. And besides the fun you will enjoy the bonuses of better health and a greater appreciation for the beauties of nature.

I don't think I ever met a fisherman who wasn't, basically, a pretty good sort of person. Maybe fishing has something to do with it!

CHAPTER II

NATURAL BAITS—HOW TO FIND, RIG AND FISH THEM

Every fishing trip teaches something new and provides fresh excitement, not only in learning more about tackle and in catching more and bigger fish, but also by revealing some of the mysteries of nature. We may sit by a stream in summer and watch a buglike little creature climb from the water onto a stone or branch where his body dries in the sun. Suddenly his body splits and he wriggles out of his dark covering to become a large, shining and colorful insect. The insect quivers as we watch him closely and, as he does so, the top of his body enlarges to form gauzelike wings. As his body fluid is pumped into the wings, they extend until suddenly we see that he has become a handsome fly—a dobsonfly, an alderfly or one of many other varieties. His wings pulsate more rapidly and, suddenly fully winged, he quickly flies away.

Millions of this fly's sisters and cousins later will lay eggs in the pond or stream. Many of the eggs will hatch, eventually to become larvae like the object we saw emerge from the water. The larva of the dobsonfly, for example, is called a "hellgrammite," and it is one of the very best baits for fish. It lives under a rock in or near the water for a year or so, growing there until instinct tells it to come into the air on a warm and sunny day to hatch into a fly such as we have seen. Many types of flies go through this cycle from egg, to nymph (as the underwater larva is called), to fly. Both the nymph and the fly are valued food for fish, so let's learn a little about them.

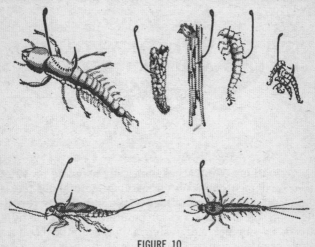

FIGURE 10
BAITS FROM A STREAM
(Hellgrammite, Caddis Cases and Nymph, and Other Nymphs)

To do this, and to get a box of bait at the same time, we'll find an old window screen. At any time during the fishing season let's take the screen (one of our friends can help us) and go to rocky, shallow rapids. Hold the screen against the bottom of the stream at an angle facing downstream so the top of the screen is barely above water. Our friend, working a few feet above us, will turn over or disturb rocks. This will dislodge whatever is underneath, including the nymphs of many species of insects such as caddisflies, dragonflies, craneflies, mayflies and stoneflies. These nymphs wash against the screen and are held by it. When several are collected, the screen is raised and whatever we've found can be picked off and put in a box of damp moss or leaves. Later, if we want to identify them, books from the library on nymphs (entomology) and nymph fishing will help us. Typical examples are shown in drawing 10. All make excellent baits on small, light hooks, whether the larvae are extracted from their cases or not. The types found in hard cases can be taken out of them and several, if necessary, can be strung on the hook.

Being about two inches long, the hellgrammite

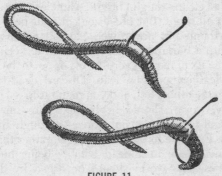

FIGURE 11
TWO WAYS OF HOOKING A WORM

(which we'll often find this way) is a tasty tidbit for big fish. When a small light wire hook is inserted under his collar, as shown (or through his tail), the hellgrammite can be fished like a worm. Many fishermen catch more and bigger fish with hellgrammites than with anything else.

WORMS

Since everybody knows how to fish worms, perhaps we should describe this only briefly. But do we know? Worm fishing is a highly skilled art; don't let fly fishermen tell you otherwise. Best results are obtained by cleansing and toughening worms after we dig them out of rich, loamy soil. We should have a tight wooden box filled with damp, fine sand. In the middle of this we should put a large mass of damp moss and compost, and spread over this a good supply of coffee grounds, corn meal and bread crumbs for food. We'll dig our worms a few days in advance and toss them onto their new home so the lively ones can dig down in. They'll cleanse and toughen themselves in the sand, and should multiply in the moss. After a few days in the worm box they'll be bright red when put on the hook, and tough enough so they won't come off easily.

Worm fishermen keep a worm box always stocked, so there'll be clean, tough, bright, slimeless worms ready for use at all times. But don't neglect your box! Keep the contents damp but never wet. Store it outdoors in the shade, with a burlap sack or two over it to keep the contents cool. Examine it every week or so to be sure the moss or leaf compost is clean. Discard dead worms, if any. Keep the others fed, and you're in business!

Usually, worms should be hooked with small, short-shank, light-wire hooks only once—through the collar, as shown. Fish like to see them wiggle, rather than seeing them bunched up in a dead ball by being hooked too many times. The worm should be fished by drifting it naturally into holes and eddies where big fish should be, so let out line when necessary and guide it into fishy looking places.

Lead should not be used unless necessary, because it deadens the natural drift of the lure. There's no harm in putting on two or three small worms, but always change them for new ones when they become inactive. And when you feel a fish working on the worm, don't pull it away from him! Give him time to swallow it (and the hook, too). When he moves off with it and you see your line going out, that's the time to strike! Otherwise, all you may get back is a wormless hook!

The drawing also shows a way to make the hook weedless when we're fishing over weed beds or near lily pads and grasses. After hooking on the worm, impale the forward (shorter) end over the barb of the hook until it conceals the barb and part of the bend of the hook.

NIGHTCRAWLERS

Since nightcrawlers usually are pretty big, let's confine their use to places where we expect to catch big fish, or fish with large mouths. Hook them, store them and fish them the same as the smaller worms. Here's a way to catch some easily:

Nightcrawlers come to the surface on nights when the

FIGURE 12
MINNOWS RIGGED FOR STILL FISHING

grass is damp. If it isn't, we can wet it down with a hose and get them to come up. We'll need a flashlight, preferably with a piece of red balloon rubber covering the lens. Crawl along on the grass, shining the dim light several feet ahead. When you spot a nightcrawler on the surface, make a stealthy but quick grab for him, because he can get back into his hole in an instant. With a good place to hunt them, and a little practice in grabbing them, the bait box should be filled in no time.

MINNOWS

Minnows (usually small ones) are one of the very best baits for most game fish. We can catch them with a fine-meshed net in quiet backwaters of streams and in similar shallow spots in ponds and lakes. But usually the easiest way is to invest in a minnow trap. These cost very little. Tackle shops can demonstrate several kinds and explain how to bait one with bread and how to tie it to a dock or branch with a long cord so it will rest on the bottom and can be pulled up easily.

When fishing with minnows, we should keep them in a minnow bucket—preferably hung by a cord in the water, because the water in the bucket must remain cool and must change itself (or be changed) frequently to prevent its losing oxygen. Warm water, or water from which the minnows have removed most of the oxygen, will cause the little fish to die. Lacking a minnow bucket, we can keep them for a short time in a pail partly full of cold water, but screening should be placed over it so the water can be poured out and renewed frequently.

Every minnow fisherman will have favorite ways of hooking minnows, and very few will agree on the best ones—but here are a few of them. In still fishing, or for casting to short distances, the minnow can be hooked through both lips, through the fleshy part of the back under the dorsal fin, or through the body near the tail. Avoid hooking him below the spine or in the body cavity because we want to keep him alive during this kind of fishing.

Let's not use lead or bobbers unless we have to, because these affect the natural action of the bait. A live minnow will try to swim to the bottom, so the trick is to let him do it, but not to let him go so deep that he will become tangled in weeds. Fishing just above the bottom, or just above the weeds, usually is the best depth; this can be controlled by the amount of line we let out. If we need to sink the minnow deeper, one or two split shot placed on line or leader a foot or two above the bait should do the job—but avoid using any more lead than necessary. If a bobber seems to be needed (we'll show how to make them later on), put it far enough up on the line or leader to keep the bait just above the bottom or above the weeds.

When trolling with minnows, or when using them for longer casts, we should rig them quite differently. A good

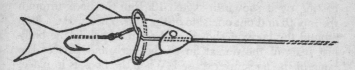

FIGURE 13
A MINNOW RIGGED FOR CASTING

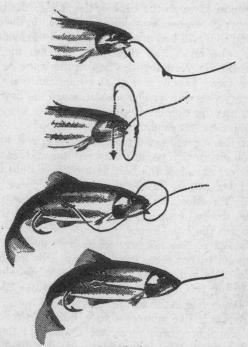

FIGURE 14
RIGGING A MINNOW FOR TROLLING

casting rig is shown in sketch 13. Run the hook through the mouth and out one side of the gills. Then make a loop around the body as shown, and set the hook in the body just back of the dorsal fin so the barb and part of the bend of the hook are exposed. When the hook is in place, carefully tighten the leader so the rig looks as in the sketch. This allows the minnow to be cast to good distances, but we'll have to work the rod with short jerks when fishing in the bait to give it lifelike action.

The rig for trolling must put a curve in the minnow so it will rotate slowly as the boat moves along. As the sketch shows, first pass the hook through the lower lip and then through the whole head from top to bottom just back of the minnow's eye. Pull some extra line (or leader) through so this can be done easily. Then hook the minnow through the back of the side of the body, as the sketch illustrates. Now, holding the bait in the palm of the hand so it will be curved slightly, pull the leader back through the head, and then back through the lip, to tighten the rig. Now test the bait in the water at proper trolling speed (about as fast as a man can walk) to be sure it revolves slowly. The revolutions of the bait can be made faster by tightening the rig to give it more curve. Loosen it a bit if it should revolve more slowly.

Since this rig will put a twist in the line, it is advisable to tie on one or two swivels between line and leader four or five feet ahead of the bait. If the line should become twisted, we can fix this by rigging a bait curved in the opposite direction. By trolling this for the same length of time, the twist should be removed. If lead is necessary to fish the bait deeper, it should be put on the line near the swivels, but not between swivels and bait.

Minnows two or three inches long usually are best, especially early in the season. Longer ones may do better for very big fish, or when the baitfish in the lake have grown larger late in the season.

If we bring live minnows to a lake or stream from which we didn't catch them, we should not dump the unused ones in the water. Many good fishing waters have been ruined by people introducing minnows which are trash fish because they can eventually multiply to the extent that they consume food which game fish need. The result of this is fewer and smaller game fish.

CRICKETS

Almost everybody knows the black or dark brown cricket which sometimes gets into houses and is supposed to bring good luck. Crickets often bring good luck to fishermen. Since these fairly large insects don't like dewy grass or rainy weather, the best place and time to look for them outdoors is under boards, logs, stones, tarpaper or other refuse in the early morning. Catch them by hand or in a net, and keep them in a small box with grass in it. Use small, light-wire hooks and hook the crickets under the collar so they will stay alive. Cast them, or drop them, in the current of a stream and let them float downstream naturally while you let out line. Sometimes fast currents will pull them underneath, but fish seem to like them either floating or deep. In pond or lake fishing, cast the crickets along the shoreline, as if they had just fallen into the water from the bank.

FIGURE 15
A CRICKET AND A GRASSHOPPER
HOOKED THROUGH THE COLLAR

GRASSHOPPERS

We fish grasshoppers just as we do crickets—and they make excellent bait when hooked and used in the same way. Since they appear late in the season, don't look for them until you see them. Then, there's an easy way to catch them. Just spread a woolly blanket on the grass wherever a lot of them are jumping around, and chase the grasshoppers onto it. Their feet will catch in the wool, so they can be picked off easily and put into a box with grass in it—the same way as you keep the crickets. Plastic boxes with sliding tops are best because you can reach in and get one insect without letting others get away. Fishing lures and hooks often come in such boxes, but any small, strong box will do. When a nylon stocking, or part of one, is put in the bottom of the box the spurs on grasshoppers' feet catch in the mesh enough to prevent them from jumping out. Punch a few holes in the box for ventilation.

Another way to collect grasshoppers is to look for them very early in the morning. They are dormant when it is cold, so they can be picked up more easily.

GRUBS

Grubs (the larvae of beetles) and various kinds of worms which live above ground also make excellent baits —leafworms, cabbage worms, corn borers, tomato worms and many other kinds. Their names often indicate where to find them, but many can be collected by turning over or breaking open rotten logs, boards or stumps. Late in the season we see goldenrod stalks with ball-like swellings on the stems. Carefully open these and you should find a grub inside. Hook these small baits through the head—using small, short-shank, light-wire hooks again. If the baits are very small, two or more can be hooked on at once.

CRAYFISH

When you see crayfish (which look like tiny lobsters) —or "crawdads," as they are called in the south—remember that these, too, make excellent baits. Sometimes they inhabit holes in the banks of streams and ponds, and they can be caught by hand by turning over rocks in or near streams, if you're quick enough. A better way is to hold a net in the water on the downstream side of the rocks you turn over. When the crayfish are forced to leave the protection of the rock, they'll drift into the net. Fish them naturally, as you do worms, grasshoppers or crickets, for example. Break off the large claws and insert the fine-wire hook under the tail, as shown in sketch 16.

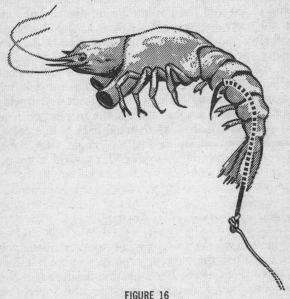

FIGURE 16
A CRAYFISH HOOKED THROUGH THE TAIL

FROGS

Other good baits are small frogs, tadpoles (pollywogs) and salamanders. Hook a frog through the thigh of a rear leg, or through the lips, and let him swim about naturally wherever you want him to. The thigh hookup is best for still fishing, the lip hookup for casting. In the latter method, if the frog is dead it makes little difference. Just skitter him around on the surface to make him look alive.

I remember that when I was a youngster my family took me to visit another family who had a cottage on a pond. I caught a sackful of frogs by putting a tiny piece of red flannel on a hook at the end of a long pole and holding it in front of the frogs I saw in the water along the bank. The frogs would hook themselves by trying to grab the flannel, and would end up in the sack. I put the sackful of frogs in the kitchen during dinner, but somehow the fastening came loose and it tipped over. So everybody tried to catch the dozens of frogs which were hopping about in the cottage, and we learned that it is much easier to catch them outdoors than it is indoors. The lady who owned the cottage stepped on one with her bare feet during the night and let out a yelp which scared everybody else as much as the frog scared her. I don't remember that we were asked back to that cottage again, but I do remember that we caught a lot of bass with some of the frogs. Anyway, if a sackful of frogs is brought into the house, remember to be sure the sack is securely tied!

TADPOLES AND SALAMANDERS

Tadpoles (which can be caught in a net) make good baits, too. Hook them through the base of the tail. Keep and carry them as you do minnows. Salamanders (like little lizards) are found in damp places near water. Grab them by the head or by the middle, because their tails are tender and might pull off. Hook them through the lips, the tail, or one of their feet. Carry frogs and salamanders in a bait bucket with a layer of moss or wet leaves on the bottom. These two baits are best when still fishing.

Now, let's get acquainted with two kinds of bait which aren't alive—strip baits and dough balls.

STRIP BAITS

Strip baits are cut from the side or belly of a fish you've caught, and any trash fish like sucker, chub or carp will do. Strips cut from the belly of a perch are excellent. The strips can be from one and a half to several inches long, and are cut and hooked as drawing 17 shows. If the fish is small, include one or all three of the lower fins on the bait, as illustrated. One fin alone sometimes works well. These can be used for trolling or for casting, but you'll have to give them lots of twitching action to make them act alive. If you are using baits like these among lily pads or grasses, it is best to use a weedless hook.

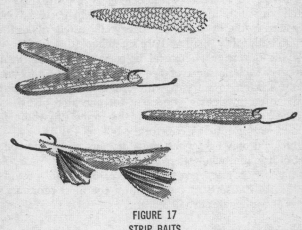

FIGURE 17
STRIP BAITS

DOUGH BALLS

Dough balls are excellent for fish such as suckers, carp, bullheads and catfish, but they aren't much good for other kinds. There are many ways to make them, and some fishermen think that the worse they smell the better they work. That's why some kinds are called "stink baits." Here are four less smelly "recipes." All of them are molded into small, stiff, compact balls, from pea to walnut size, and are put on the hook so it is hidden as much as possible inside the ball:

Mix equal parts of bread, oatmeal, cereal and sugar with enough water to make a stiff dough.

Mix equal parts of hamburger steak and cheese with flour and enough water so that, when kneaded well, it will make a stiff paste.

Cut a white, pink or yellow plastic sponge into small cubes and work a lot of cheese spread into them.

Mix flour and cheese into firm balls.

Dough balls usually are fished merely by letting them lie on the bottom. Sooner or later one of the above kinds of fish will come along and pick them up—if you're fishing in the right place. Use small balls if you expect to catch small fish and larger ones for the bigger fish; but, if you're in doubt about the size you'll catch, make the dough balls fairly small and use small hooks.

These dozen or so natural baits are not all of them, but they include most of the important ones—and certainly enough to start in with. Almost any small thing that moves provides a good bait for one kind of fish or another, and many of them can be found anywhere in woods, waters or fields, free for the taking.

But, you may ask, what kinds of bait are best for one sort of fish, and what other kinds for other sorts? The following list isn't the complete menu, but it will provide an idea of the sorts of bait some of the most prominent types of fresh water fish like best:

TROUT (all kinds)

Small trout are insect eaters and, later in this book, we'll learn how to take them (and many other species) with artificial flies because most fishermen think this is the greatest part of the sport of fishing. But as far as nat-

FIGURE 18
TROUT

ural baits are concerned, worms are the most popular, except that big trout also go for minnows because they are more of a "square meal." Nymphs, hellgrammites, grubs, crickets, grasshoppers, salamanders and crayfish are all good. So are strip baits. It's fun to experiment with the various kinds.

SMALLMOUTH BASS

These sporty game fish are found in rocky streams, ponds and lakes, in cold, deep water over ledges and rocky bottoms, in weed beds and deep pools, near stumps and docks, and close to steep rocky dropoffs. In the eve-

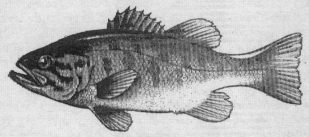

FIGURE 19
SMALLMOUTH BASS

ning they often come into shallow water among lily pads and grasses to find food, and sometimes can be located by their splashing. They like small baits such as nymphs (especially hellgrammites), grubs, crickets, crayfish, leeches and worms. Since smallmouth bass enjoy cold water, they often share pools in streams with trout, and often are caught with the same baits or lures.

LARGEMOUTH BASS

This fish enjoys warm, fairly shallow shaded water among lily pads and grasses along the shore, around stumps and submerged logs, over weed beds or ledges, and in coves of ponds and warm water lakes. He likes

FIGURE 20
LARGEMOUTH BASS

big baits and will devour almost anything, including other fish, salamanders, frogs, minnows, worms, mice, crayfish and even birds. Hellgrammites, leeches and nightcrawlers also are good baits for largemouth bass. Strip baits and pork-rind lures are special favorites.

When fishing for largemouths, avoid making noise in the boat. Let it drift quietly while casting around stumps, lily pads and other good hiding places. When fishing on the surface, let the cast bait rest a minute or two, then work it in slowly with frequent pauses. When least expected, a big bass may splash up and take it. When they won't take baits on the surface, try fishing them deep, even if you get hung up occasionally and have to break off a few hooks.

PICKEREL

Pickerel mainly are pond fish and usually are found where there are bass. The baits for largemouth bass also

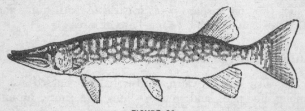

FIGURE 21
PICKEREL

are favorites for pickerel, and we fish for them in the same way.

PERCH

These usually inhabit fairly warm waters in ponds or lakes over weed beds. Since they have small mouths, small baits are best. They are great worm stealers, but there's a way to outguess them on this. Pinch a small split shot on a short, light-wire hook just back of the eye of the hook. Then thread on one end of a worm so most

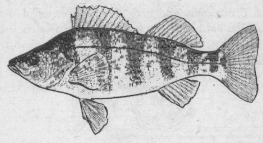

FIGURE 22
PERCH

of it is on the hook. Jig this (with short, quick up-and-down motions of the rod) over weed beds, and you should catch perch! Also, use very small minnows—my favorite, in this case. Perch will take other small natural baits, including hellgrammites and small crayfish. In trolling, use a small spinner ahead of a hook baited with a worm or minnow. Troll fairly fast, and pause occasionally to let the bait sink a little.

WALLEYES (Walleyed pike)

These large members of the perch family are among the finest of all fish to eat. They travel in schools in the deep, clear waters of many lakes and rivers and take baits easily. Fish near the bottom, preferably with minnows but also with hellgrammites, nightcrawlers or

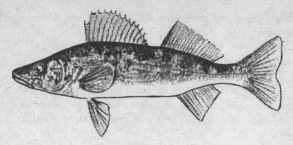

FIGURE 23
WALLEYE

worms. Fish slowly and give walleyes plenty of time to swallow the bait. The best fishing usually is after the sun has gone down.

FIGURE 24
BLUEGILL

BLUEGILLS (Bream)

This pretty and spunky little panfish likes quiet weedy water in warm ponds, and often is found in the shadow of docks and overhanging shade. Since he primarily is an insect feeder, grubs and nymphs make excellent bait. So do worms, or parts of them. The bigger bluegills like crickets and grasshoppers, too.

CRAPPIE (Calico bass)

Somewhat similar to the bluegill, crappie often grow bigger and are one of the most popular panfish, especially in southern waters. Since he has a fairly large mouth, he feeds on bait such as minnows, worms, grass-hoppers, crickets and crayfish. He also eats insects found in or on the water, so if the larger baits don't get results, try smaller ones such as grubs and nymphs. Both

FIGURE 25
CRAPPIE

the black crappie and the white crappie enjoy quiet waters containing considerable aquatic growth. They can be caught by trolling with small minnows or by still fishing with any of the above baits near the surface or deeper down. If it were put to a vote, probably most fishermen would say that small minnows are the most popular bait.

SUNFISH

This is the name for a group of small panfish which includes the pumpkinseed and the bluegill. We find them where we find bluegills, and we fish for them in the same ways.

BULLHEADS (Horned pout)

Where there's one there's usually many of them—often on or near the muddy and weedy bottom of warm-water ponds. A way to make a "fishing hole" for bullheads is to find where a few collect and throw several big meaty bones into the water where we plan to fish. In a day or two plenty of bullheads should be around. Dough balls or any kind of meat or fish are good baits for bullheads, and the "riper" they are, the better. Let the bait lie on the bottom until a fish takes it. Best fishing usually is on rainy or cloudy days, or at night. Worms also are good

FIGURE 26
SUNFISH

bait. In this case we can string as many on the hook as it will hold. When we catch and land a bullhead, usually he will shake off the hook, so the same bait can be used several times. All the baits listed for bass will take bull-heads, and so will the entrails of chickens and other small animals. In short, bullheads will eat just about anything, and the deader it is, the better they seem to like it.

CATFISH

The bullhead is a member of the catfish family, and we fish for most species of catfish in similar ways and

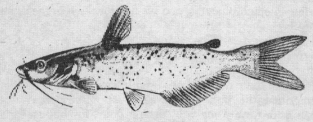

FIGURE 27
CATFISH

with the same baits as we do for him. Catfish are found in clear, unpolluted water with or without current. The bottom of the tail race of a large dam is a favorite spot. Some of the species grow very large—even as large as a hundred pounds. Since the very big ones are found in relatively few areas, and specialized methods are required for catching them, let's leave it to other books to describe this.

CARP

The common goldfish is a specially bred species of carp. Many waters contain carp where they are not wanted, because someone was thoughtless enough to lib-

FIGURE 28
CARP

erate the contents of the family goldfish bowl into them. Some people enjoy eating carp; others do not. Usually the best time to catch them is in late spring or early summer in shallow, weedy, quiet places in lakes and in still pools in streams. Carp more or less are vegetarians, and can be caught with dough balls or by stringing cooked corn, beans, peas, berries or similar food on a hook and letting the bait lie on the bottom until one of the fish picks it up and swallows it. The hook should be concealed in the bait. Carp are fun to catch because they are not timid, and a quiet fisherman usually can see what he's fishing for. They fight fairly well on light tackle, and most conservationists encourage fishing for them to get rid of them. Occasionally they can be taken with worms.

CHUB

While usually thought of as a trash fish in this country, the chub is considered a game fish in many European areas. He inhabits quietly flowing rivers and streams where fishermen often catch him on flies or baits when they expect to be catching trout. Baits for chub include dough balls, worms, grubs, bread pellets and soft cheese, but chub also will take minnows, crayfish, caterpillars and many other baits we have mentioned for other fish. They aren't fussy about what they eat; they fight fairly well on light tackle, and fishermen are doing conservation a good turn by helping to rid the streams of them. This, unfortunately, is a lost cause in most places because chub are multiplying everywhere in waters which used to be favorites for trout. This, of course, is at the expense of the trout.

SUCKERS

This is a bottom feeder related to the chub, and also usually is thought of as a trash fish although he is considered edible by many people. He inhabits quiet warm water areas in streams, ponds and lakes, where he sucks up ooze on plants, rocks, and on the bottom to obtain larvae and other edible material. He will take worms, dough balls and some of the bits of vegetable we have mentioned as baits for carp. While small suckers sometimes provide food for game fish, the larger ones compete with sport fish to the extent that they deplete sport fishing, and thus they usually are considered undesirable.

Conservationists generally regret that fishermen prefer sport fish such as trout and bass to the extent that they rarely bother trying for so-called trash fish such as carp, chub and suckers. Since there are so many of the latter, if we are fishing for fun maybe it's more fun to catch a lot of them than to run the risk of getting skunked while trying for more difficult and less prevalent species such as trout and bass. After all, carp, chubs and suckers fight quite well on the end of a line, and we are sure to make up in quantity for what may be lacking in quality!

Now, if you've read only this far, and have decided to go fishing with homemade tackle and the natural baits which are so easy to find, let's remember two of the little fine points we'll learn more about later. When in doubt about the right size of hook, use the smaller one. If in doubt about the weight of hooks, use the lighter one. If it's a decision between hooks with short and with long shanks, select the shorter one.

Secondly, when using a strong line, use a few feet of very light leader between line and hook—even if the line be monofilament. For the smaller fish in open water, leaders down to two pounds test or so will be less visible to fish, and thus will tempt more strikes than heavier leaders would. If in doubt, test a very light leader and see how strong it is. Very probably it's quite strong enough—and you'll catch more fish when using it!

CHAPTER III

WHAT HOOK—AND WHY?

What is the most important part of a set of fishing tackle? The rod? No. Although fine rods afford better casting and more safety and fun in catching fish, we can do pretty well with a simple fishpole cut from a green sapling. The reel, then? No, again, because the reel's basic purpose is merely to store line. Well, how about the line? The line is as important as the rod and the reel, but usually it is more than strong enough, and many other kinds of lines probably would cast as well.

This leaves the hook—and no matter what kind of fishing we're doing, we can't hook and hold fish consistently and safely without a good hook. Just "any old hook" won't do!

Hooks are the cheapest part of the tackle, and probably the most misunderstood. They all may look pretty much alike, but they can be as different as diamonds and glass. Hooks are the most important part of a set of fishing tackle. If anybody has any doubt about it, think of the alibis so many fishermen make when they try to excuse themselves for a luckless day out fishing.

For example, take our good friend Mortimer Addlepate. (There are millions of people just like him.) Mortimer owns several expensive glass rods, with reels and lines to fit them. He has a big tackle box bulging with lures, flies and other equipment. The guy is loaded, except that he's a bit short on fishhooks, and he wants to catch a mess of crappies for dinner.

So Mortimer goes sailing into his local sporting goods store and says, "Gimme a box of hooks—yes, that size is okay." This takes only a few minutes, and Mortimer is pleased that he got a "bargain"—more than a dollar's worth for only 79 cents!

Well, Mortimer comes home that night with only three or four crappies and a whole string of excuses. "Had a lot of hits," he says, "but they all struck short. Hooked a few, but the hook pulled out. Had a big one on, but he straightened the hook and got away."

Then Mortimer adds that the chap he went fishing with hooked every fish that took the bait, landed every one of them, and came home with his limit. "Gosh, but that guy is always lucky!" he says.

The fact is that the big "hook bargain" that poor old Mortimer fell for resulted in a box of cheap, inefficient hooks that didn't "hook and hold" as good hooks should do. So Uncle Mortimer saved about fifty cents and spoiled several days of fishing. The chap with him who got his limit bought his hooks by brand name and he paid the price for top quality. He also examined the hooks carefully to be sure they had the characteristics all good bait hooks should have—the barb in line with the eye of the hook, and the bend *double offset* for greater penetration and holding power (among a few other things very important to remember).

Expert fishermen are fussier in selecting hooks than in selecting any other element of their tackle. Good hooks make all the difference between success and poor results —so let's learn a little about fishhooks and how to choose the best ones.

Fishhooks have been vital food furnishers for centuries. The old-timers made them of bone, stone, shell, thorns or what-have-you, until they learned to fashion crude ones from metal. Modern hooks were born in Redditch, England, about the year 1560, because Redditch was an important needle manufacturing region—and the father of the modern hook was the needle. Until the early 1900's, hooks mainly were produced in England and in the Scandinavian countries. Good ones still are, but along about World War I modern American technology

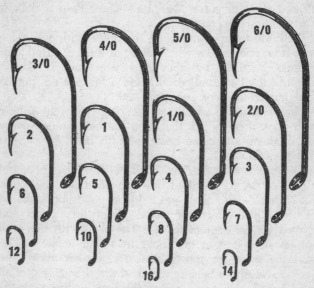

FIGURE 29
CHART OF HOOK SIZES
(Actual Size)

made old-fashioned guesswork obsolete, and hook-making headquarters moved to the USA.

Guesswork in hook design and production still prevails in some places—more than you might think. Without scientific know-how, craftsmen had to guess at correct steel formulas and at heat treating and tempering methods with the hope that the batch would result in hooks neither too brittle nor too soft. Their guesses usually were good, but they were not infallible. You'd get excellent hooks in one batch and perhaps very poor ones in another. Here and there, you still do.

Correct design is as important as correct manufacture,

and there are many designs suitable for various types of fish and for various angling methods. In the famous English book published in 1870, author H. C. Pennell said that the four most important elements of hooks are penetration, holding power, strength, and lightness plus neatness. He said, "The greatest penetrating power of a hook occurs when the line of penetration is coincident with the direction of the force applied." He was dead right, as we shall see. He developed the Pennell hook to overcome shortcomings of other designs, but he made the error of curving both the point and the lower tip section inward, pointing to the eye. This was correct in theory, but resulted in inferior hooking power.

This problem later was solved by two American craftsmen named S. M. Wright and A. D. McGill, who have enjoyed much less credit than they deserve for designing a hook which is as close to perfection as any we have today. Wright and McGill overcame the faults of the Pennell design by leaving the spear (the "bite" or lower tip section) parallel to the shank, and by curving only the point inward, pointing toward the eye, in the form of what they called an "Eagle Claw." In the opinions of millions of fishermen, Eagle Claw hooks have far better penetration and holding power than any other hooks made anywhere in the world.

Wright and McGill improved their Eagle Claw design in several other ways. The point is mechanically hollow ground for quicker penetration. The barb is cut at an an-

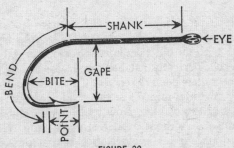

FIGURE 30
NAMES OF PARTS OF A FISHHOOK

gle which bites less deeply into the wire, thus resulting in fewer broken barbs. Since nearly 95 percent of hooks are used in bait fishing, many Wright & McGill hooks are "kirbed" or offset in a novel way. The bend is *double offset*, half on either side of the shank, thus making the hook twist into the cartilage of a fish to further increase penetration and holding power. In addition, many are partially flattened or forged on the sides for extra strength. Finally, Mr. Wright and Mr. McGill developed machines and heat-treating and tempering equipment which were far superior to any before known.

These hook improvements sparked a thriving business in Denver, Colorado, named the Wright & McGill Company, which is the exclusive manufacturer of the famous Eagle Claw hook design—a name now also given to excellent rods, reels and lines sold by the same firm. These improvements also resulted in the imposing fact that Wright & McGill Company makes and sells well over a million hooks every day—and every batch of hooks is inspected to insure perfection.

But, most important, this design does what we now know an efficient hook always should do. It puts the line of penetration in the direct line of pull, thus making it "hook and hold." It helps to eliminate short strikes and lightly hooked fish. It lets modern fishermen return home with heavier creels and fewer excuses. All this may be helpful news to our "luckless" friend, Mortimer Addlepate, and to many others who think that a hook is just a hook!

To prove these facts about the relative hooking and holding powers of various types of hooks, let's try an experiment with an old telephone directory or a big catalog. Select a perfectly flat hook and also a double-offset hook such as has been described. Tie each one to a piece of leader material and place them side by side between the pages of the catalog. Now, pull out the flat hook. It may come out without even tearing a page. Then pull out the double-offset hook. Notice that it digs into the pages so that pulling it out probably is impossible! The

FIGURE 31
A WAY TO TEST HOOKING AND
HOLDING POWER OF A FISHHOOK

same thing often would happen in fishing when these hooks are between the jaws of a fish.

To show the difference between the Eagle Claw hook (where the point is curved in line of pull) and other types (where the point is not curved in line of pull), stick the point of the Eagle Claw, tied to a short leader, into a bar of soap and then pull it through the bar. The

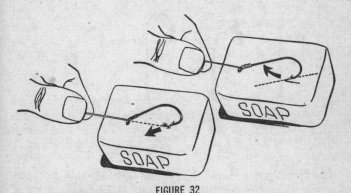

FIGURE 32
A WAY TO TEST THE PENETRATION OF A FISHHOOK
(Point of top hook is not curved in line of pull. The lower hook's point is curved in line of pull.)

greater penetration of this type is obvious when the same experiment is made with the other types.

What about the types of hooks to select for various purposes? Without getting bogged down in detail, let's look quickly at eight of the well-known patterns to see which ones we should select for various types of fishing.

SPROAT: This is a parabolic bend hook with a straight point. It is one of the best and strongest early designs for fresh water fishing and often is used for dressing wet flies. When made with light wire it is an excellent dry fly hook.

MODEL PERFECT: Ideal for dressing both wet and

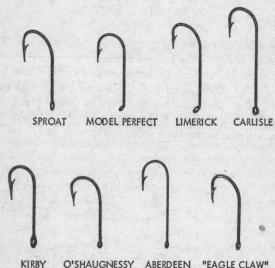

SPROAT   MODEL PERFECT   LIMERICK   CARLISLE

KIRBY   O'SHAUGNESSY   ABERDEEN   "EAGLE CLAW"

FIGURE 33
SOME POPULAR HOOK DESIGNS

dry flies. It is a perfectly round-bend all-purpose hook with a wide gap, and usually is made of light wire.

LIMERICK: This hook has a half-round parabolic bend with a straight point designed for superior strength. It is excellent for dressing nymphs and wet flies when a heavier hook is needed. Its design in long-shanked sizes makes it very popular for dressing streamer flies and bucktails.

KIRBY: This round-bend hook is similar to the Sproat except that the point is offset or "kirbed" for better penetration. This directs penetration at an angle with the shank to help prevent fish from shaking loose. The Kirby was used mainly for bait fishing before the superior Eagle Claw was designed for the same purpose.

O'SHAUGNESSY: This resembles the Sproat and Limerick except that its point is bent slightly outward. It usually is made of heavy wire for extra strength. Fishermen prefer it for dressing heavy wet flies and for bait fishing for heavy-mouthed slow-biting fish. It also is excellent for trotline fishing.

ABERDEEN: This hook has a slightly squared round bend with extra width between point and shank so that, when baited with a minnow, its point will extend out of the fish rather than being imbedded in the bait. Its light wire avoids excessive puncturing, thus keeping the bait fish alive longer. It also is a good light-wire nymph hook. It is made to bend before breaking, and thus is easily retrieved from snags.

CARLISLE: This round-bend hook has an extra long shank and a straight offset point. It is especially designed for minnow and nightcrawler fishing because its length helps to prevent the fish from swallowing the hook.

EAGLE CLAW: Often termed the greatest modern improvement for hooking and holding fish, this American design correctly provides a direct line of pull by the point's being curved inward in line with the eye. Because this hook also has several other improvements which have been discussed, it undoubtedly is the world's most popular design for bait fishing. It also is used for dressing flies and for attachment to other types of lures. Hooks of this design are made both with and without the double-offset feature, in singles, doubles and trebles—plus bait-holder and snelled types.

Snelled hooks come with the leader already attached, usually having been passed down through the upturned eye and tied securely around the shank. This holds the hook directly in line with the leader, thus giving it more positive hooking qualities. The opposite end is tied into a loop to make it easier and faster to change hooks. Snelled hooks usually are tied with the correct pound test of leader for the size of the hook, thus eliminating guesswork for the beginner. The knots at hook and loop of reputable brands are properly and securely tied. The snelled hook, with its short leader, is ideal for use with heavier, nontransparent lines, such as braided lines, heavy trolling lines and trotlines.

All this gives us several yardsticks to go by in hook selection. We know in a general way what design of hook to select for the type of fishing we plan to do, and we know we can get this design in favorite sizes, lengths, strengths and finishes, not only in single hooks but usually also in doubles, trebles and weedless designs. We know why we should select well-known brands, be they of American or of foreign manufacture. We know what types of hooks hook and hold most securely, and what types don't do nearly as well. We know why modern technological equipment plays such an important part in producing high-quality hooks.

Finally, let's remember two more important tips. No matter how efficient the hook is when you buy it, it can't do its best to help catch fish unless its point is kept needle sharp. Carry a small honing stone to touch up the point as often as it needs it. A small flat file is even better, if the hooks are large. Tie it to the leader with the proper knot, and be sure the leader is straight, with no coils or kinks in it. A three-inch (or so) square of inner-tube rubber is excellent for this purpose. Double the square between your fingers and pull the leader through it under moderate pressure until the kinks and coils smooth out.

Hooks often are neglected, perhaps because they are among the least expensive elements of tackle. Nevertheless, they are the most important. Anglers who understand about them, and who use them properly, are the ones who catch the "big ones." The others come home without these trophies, and try to explain why "The Big One" got away!

CHAPTER IV

THE FIRST FISHING OUTFIT

A homemade fishpole, a dog, a pleasant day and a woodsy brook with some fish in it make a combination I hope every young person can enjoy even more often than I did when I was a child. But the time comes when interest in the homemade pole wears out, unless we have to make one for emergency use. We want something better—a real store-bought set of fishing tackle all our own.

When I was a kid, selection wasn't much of a problem because spinning and spin-casting tackle and the beautiful glass rods we have today hadn't been invented—or at least we didn't know about them. The choice was either fly-fishing tackle or a plug-casting outfit, and split bamboo rods were as popular then as glass rods are today.

So I decided on a fly rod, with a reel, line and leaders to fit it, and I mowed lawns and shoveled crushed rock for several weeks to earn what they cost. A friend showed me how to use the tackle. He insisted that I should fish with flies instead of live bait, because he thought that artificial flies were sportier and more fun and that they caught more fish. At first I wasn't convinced of this, and put on a worm or some other live bait occasionally. But I soon learned it was more fun to cast a fly, and that my instructor was right when he said flies usually caught more fish than could be caught with bait.

Probably most fishermen shy away from fly fishing because they think it is too complicated and too hard to learn. They think they have to be able to cast to long distances when, actually, nearly all fly fishing can be done within a radius of twenty-five feet or so. Thus, with even a middling good fly-fishing outfit, anyone can learn in a few minutes to cast to that distance, or farther, if he merely is able to raise and lower his forearm properly. We'll learn about that in the next chapter but, right now, let's explode the myth that fly fishing is difficult. Anybody can do it!

In selecting our first fishing outfit we need to know the good and bad points about each type of tackle: fly casting, spinning, spin casting and plug casting. Each type will be described in future chapters, but these comments may help you decide which one should be chosen for the first outfit.

FLY CASTING:

This is the only one of the four methods by which we can successfully cast unweighted artificial flies—because in fly fishing we cast the line rather than the lure. Since the line is thick enough to have weight in it, it can cast

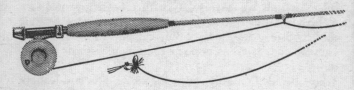

FIGURE 34
A FLY-CASTING OUTFIT

nearly weightless lures almost effortlessly. On the other hand, it cannot cast heavier lures as well as can be done by the other three methods.

A fly-casting outfit is ideal for fishing wet flies, dry flies, artificial nymphs, or streamers and bucktails. This includes a tremendous range of traditional lures which are considered by fly fishermen to be the sportiest and most productive for catching almost all varieties of fresh-water fish.

The average fly-casting outfit also is excellent for handling small bass bugs, including the slightly bulky but light varieties dressed with cork or hair bodies. This same outfit is good for casting light baits such as very small minnows, worms, grasshoppers, crickets, grubs, salamanders, very small frogs, small strip baits, small dough balls and other lures which have very little bulk or weight. In this class we also can include tiny wobbling spoons and spinners, plus very light spinner-and-fly or spinner-and-bait combinations.

This includes such a wide range of lures that, under most conditions, a fly-casting outfit is essential for fishermen, regardless of whatever other types of tackle they might own. However, the more weight the lure has, the less suitable it is for fly casting. Adding even one small split shot to a fly or lure decreases the efficiency and fun of using this type of tackle; but, with any of the lures mentioned above, it does not decrease efficiency and fun to the extent that it is impractical.

When we get to lures of any sort which have appreciable weight, such as a quarter of an ounce or more, we are getting out of the fly-casting range and into the ranges of the other three types of tackle.

In considering a fly-casting outfit, we also should consider the conditions under which we'll be doing most of our fishing. A fly-casting outfit is excellent for trolling (but not for casting) when we are using somewhat heavier lures than those mentioned above. For example, if we are fishing in brushy places, where our back cast often would get hung up in trees or bushes, a fly-fishing outfit can be a disadvantage except in the hands of experts. This also is true when casting in the wind, and when very long casts are necessary. In such cases one of the other types of outfit probably would be preferable.

SPINNING

This type of tackle came into prominence shortly after World War II and has been extremely popular ever since. The idea behind it is that monofilament line (and light braided line, in some cases) can be cast off a fixed (nonrevolving), open-faced (no cover) spool easier and to longer distances than with any other type of tackle when weighted lures are used. This is because all possi-

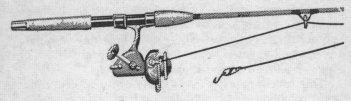

FIGURE 35
A SPINNING OUTFIT

ble friction is eliminated. To test this theory, hold a spool of thread by one end and pull the thread off the other end. It comes off in a spiral with much less friction than if the spool were made to revolve in pulling it off. For this reason, small, compact weighted lures can be cast easier and to longer distances than with any of the other three types of tackle.

Another point in favor of spinning (and of spin casting) is freedom from backlash—which can be quite common and very bothersome in plug casting. However, even if we don't get backlashes, we will get snarls if the line isn't kept tight on the reel spool at all times. When line on the reel is loose, one tight coil will pull off other loose coils in a bunch. These will catch and knot together when passing through the rod guides, thus resulting in snarls. There is no reason for this to happen if the line is kept tight on the spool, and if the spool is not overloaded with line. If it does happen, it is because the fisherman is careless with his tackle or, in rare cases, because something is wrong with his reel.

What weights of lures should be used? Generally, for fresh water fishing, lures in the one-quarter-ounce range are ideal with lines testing from three to six pounds in strength. Lighter lures call for ultralight tackle, which is is not recommended for beginners. Heavier lures, of one-half ounce or more, require heavy spinning tackle. With such lures spin-casting or plug-casting tackle might be better.

The ideal weight range for lures with average strength spinning tackle is between one-fourth and one-half an ounce. Spinning, even with heavy gear, is not designed for lures weighing over an ounce and a half—and these heavy lures generally are confined to salt-water fishing or, in fresh water, for muskellunge, big pike or other whoppers.

Spinning tackle (like spin-casting and plug-casting tackle) is excellent for long casts with weighted lures, especially when it is too windy for fly fishing and when there are obstructions behind the fisherman which would interfere with fly fishing. It also is excellent when we have to go deep to catch fish.

Spinning tackle is ideal for casting weighted spinners, wobbling spoons, jigs, plugs of all types, other heavy artificial lures, minnows, nightcrawlers and other natural baits in the weight range we have discussed. This includes a tremendous range of lures suitable for use on the surface and at almost any depth.

If people have trouble with spinning gear, it is because they don't know how to use it. It is a simple method, but it does require knowledge easily found in magazine articles and in books. (This book will provide the essentials.) It has been said that spinning is easier to learn than fly fishing. This may be so if we want to be an expert in either method but, from an elementary standpoint, I don't think it is. The value of spinning is that, with the tackle, one can cast small, compact, weighted lures farther and easier than with any other method.

SPIN CASTING

Spin casting is a development of the spinning method which often is confused with spinning. While the two are somewhat similar, they also are in other ways quite different. A spin-casting reel also is a fixed-spool reel from which the line uncoils in a manner similar to that of a spinning reel. However, the spin-casting reel is equipped with a cover, or hood, which conceals the line. The line emerges from a small hole, or eyelet, in the center of the hood. For this reason the spin-casting reel casts with more friction than the spinning reel—which makes it less suitable for casting very light lures to long distances. In casting, the line is released by a thumb trigger, and it is retrieved by a device which revolves as the handle is turned. For most accurate casting I believe that the spinning method is superior.

Perhaps the decision between spinning and spin casting lies in how often the fisherman will use plugs and other lures which should be fished in with very jerky

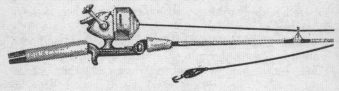

FIGURE 36
A SPIN-CASTING OUTFIT

retrieves. Spinning tackle works best with a fairly steady retrieve, because this winds the line back evenly on the spool. A very jerky retrieve with spinning tackle can cause the combination of tight and loose coils which result in the snarls we mentioned. Spin-casting tackle (and plug-casting tackle) is much less inclined to do this. Consequently, if we usually plan to fish plugs with the extremely erratic retrieves sometimes so necessary in filling the creel, we may find that a spin-casting outfit is the best choice.

Spin-casting reels are made in many designs, most of which can be used either with a spinning rod or a plug-casting rod. We probably would start an argument if we should say that spin casting is easier than spinning, but the great number of spin-casting reels being sold indicates that millions of people think it is, or that it works better for the reasons just mentioned.

In the author's opinion, spin casting is a method in between spinning and plug casting. It calls for the heavier lures that plug casters usually use, and it has the advantage of freedom from backlash that plug casters often find so troublesome.

PLUG CASTING

Undoubtedly some people will say that this method should be called "bait casting," but this term is a relic of the 1800's when this type of tackle was used almost exclusively for casting bait. It now no longer seems appro-

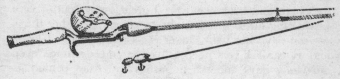

FIGURE 37
A PLUG-CASTING OUTFIT

priate because most of its use is with plugs. It differs from spinning and spin casting in that it calls for a revolving spool reel used with the shorter 4½ to 5½ foot recessed-handle rods currently also often used in spin casting.

Plug-casting advocates, of which there still are many, evidently think this method is more accurate for casting, and that the multiplying reel works better in handling the erratic rod action necessary for alternate slow and fast reeling and the energetic popping and manipulation of plugs and baits which often is the secret of getting the maximum number of strikes. However, when beginners attempt this type of casting they are sure to get frequent and troublesome backlashes. The result is that they often spend more time untangling line than they do in fishing. Thus, a large percentage get rid of this tackle and turn to less troublesome methods.

Lures for plug fishing list in the thousands and include spinners, wobblers, jigs and bait, as well as plugs. Among the various types of plugs are designs for popping and skittering on the surface, floating-diving plugs of various types, and deep-running models. Usually they are in the one-half-ounce range.

To summarize all this, we find that two different outfits are necessary to cover a broad range of fresh water fishing. One is a fly-casting outfit and the other is a choice between spinning, spin casting and plug casting. Which one we choose for our first fishing outfit depends on where we live, the most interesting kinds of fishing available there, and what kind of tackle we think we most would enjoy. If this choice is a fly-fishing outfit, it should be ideal for little brooks and streams as well as for ponds and lakes—and for a great assortment of very fascinating lures. If it is a choice among the other three, we can have fun with longer casts with weighted lures, and we can fish very deep as well as on the surface, even on windy days and when bushes and trees behind us might affect successful fly fishing.

CARE OF TACKLE

Since this is a general discussion of tackle, let's include a few tips on how to take care of it, because proper care will extend its usefulness amazingly.

Glass rods need little care except to keep them clean, which can be done with a wet, soapy cloth. Before assembling the rod, rub the male ferrule in your hair or against your nose to oil it slightly. Never use machine oil, because too much or too heavy oil will increase suction and make the ferrules difficult to pull apart. If the male ferrule can't be seated properly, dirt or corrosion may be the cause. Polish the male ferrule, and use a folded pipe cleaner and a little lighter fluid to swab out the inside of the female one. Check rod windings for indications that they might be starting to fray. If so, put a drop of lacquer on your finger and rub the winding lightly to coat it. In some cases two or three applications may be advisable.

If the rod is difficult to disassemble, always use a pulling motion rather than a twisting one. If one person can't pull it apart, two people, each with a hand above and below the ferrule, usually can. Another way is to sit down, hold the rod above and below the ferrule with wrists placed just outside of your knees, and use the leverage of your knees to aid the strength of your arms. On the rare occasions when ferrules stick badly, of course they should be cleaned.

Fish slime and dirt on rod grips do no harm except for appearance. A soapy scrub brush should clean the grip nicely. Fine wire soap pads also will do it, but avoid using the coarse ones.

Reels rarely get out of order except by being damaged, but they need cleaning and oiling occasionally. Remove spools of fly reels from the housing; clean the inside with a slightly oily cloth or a small brush, and add a bit of vaseline or reel grease to the gears. The more complicated reels should be handled as the instructions which come with them specify, so always save the instruction folders.

Mechanically inclined fishermen who feel competent to disassemble complicated reels find it handy to use an egg carton in which to put parts in order of their disassembly. This prevents losing small parts and indicates which ones should be put back on first.

Spinning and plug-casting lines can be left on reel spools indefinitely. After storage, monofilament lines may be stiff and wiry. To make them limp again, attach the forward end by a fish hook to a stump or branch and walk backward until the castable line is off the reel. A pull or two will remove stiffness and also test the line for weak spots.

Fly lines need more care. Most fishermen remove them from the reels at the end of the season, coil them loosely and hang them in a plastic bag in a cool dark closet until the next season. If they become sticky, a rubbing with talcum powder should help. Periodic rubbings with line dressing as often as necessary keep the lines pliant.

Let's not throw away broken lures, because we'll explain in Chapter XI how to fix them and how to make new lures from old or broken ones. Unpainted spoons and spinners whose blades become corroded can be polished with mud, crocus cloth or metal polish. While polished lures can be varnished to prevent tarnish, dull ones may catch more fish on bright days or when the water is low—so let's polish them only when necessary and let's avoid lacquering them. A small piece of crocus cloth (like extremely fine sandpaper) can be carried in the tackle box and will restore the desired brightness in seconds.

One of the most important things in tackle care is to check the sharpness of hooks frequently. Remove rust and touch up barbs and points. Damaged hooks should be discarded where bare feet and animals can't come in contact with them.

CHAPTER V

FLY CASTING IS EASY!

Many people never start to enjoy fly fishing because of the tremendous amount of information they think they must learn about it. Well, there *is* a lot to learn, but we don't have to know everything all at once. Like baseball or football or any other sport, we get into the game to enjoy it, and we improve as we go along. If it were too easy it wouldn't be nearly as much fun.

So let's try to make this chapter on fly casting just as simple as we can. When we know and practice what's in it, we'll be fly fishermen. We'll be able to cast smoothly to reasonable distances with appropriate tackle, and we'll catch fish. After that, we can look forward to a lifetime of fun in improving our skill and knowledge.

Buying the right kind of tubular glass rod is very important, along with the right size of line to bring out its action. Avoid no-name "bargains," because a cheaply made rod which won't cast well may look very similar to a brand name one which is expertly built to deliver maximum power and accuracy. Glass rods are relatively inexpensive, so invest an extra dollar or two to get one which makes casting easy and effortless. To do this, choose from famous brands such as Heddon, Shakespeare, True Temper, Eagle Claw (Wright & McGill) and other prominent names. All anglers have preferences. Mine is for Eagle Claw rods, because I have seen them made and know the infinite care and value which goes into them. They cast so beautifully that I usually use them in preference to expensive ones. A respected brand name is a guarantee of quality, but buying an unknown brand is like buying a "pig in a poke."

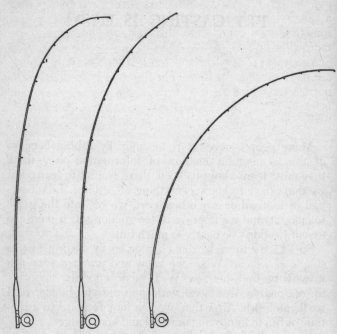

FAST ACTION   MEDIUM ACTION   SOFT ACTION

FIGURE 38

TYPES OF FLY ROD ACTIONS

("Soft action" is undesirable because such a rod is too soft in the butt. "Fast action" is typical of rods too soft in the tip. "Medium action" provides longest and most accurate casts; is sometimes called "parabolic action.")

Upon finding a rod whose size, price and appearance seem appealing, hold the tip against the ceiling and push up on it a little to be sure the action is progressively distributed from butt to tip. This "medium" action should resemble one side of a parabola, except that it has slightly more action at the tip to make it more suitable for both wet and dry fly fishing, as drawing 38 shows. This action, incidentally, is found in Wright & McGill tubular glass rods—which evidently is one reason why they are so popular. Avoid the type that has a very wiggly tip and a heavy butt which flexes very little. These weak tips sometimes are called "fast tips," but they make casting more difficult.

Also avoid rods which are too long or too short. There are good reasons for these, but they are specialized rods not recommended for the beginner. Usually an 8-foot rod is an ideal all-around one for a man, and a 7½-foot rod for ladies and young people.

Fly rods come in a choice of two, three or four sections. If the length of the disassembled rod is no problem in transportation, select a two-section one because it has one less set of ferrules to bother with. Ferrules usually do more harm than good in fly rod action, so the fewer the better. However, for back-packing and when carrying a rod on hikes, a very short one is most helpful because

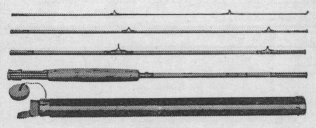

FIGURE 39
THE "TRAILMASTER" FOUR-PIECE FLY ROD FITS
INTO A CASE ONLY 24 INCHES LONG!

it is less inclined to catch on branches—especially when being carried in a pack.

Somewhat against his better judgment, the author bought a four-section Trailmaster rod made by the Eagle Claw people. This, in its case, is less than 24 inches long, so is easy to pack on wilderness trips. I thought that, being in four sections, it wouldn't cast very well, but the amazing thing is that it casts beautifully! It vividly illustrates how well high-quality manufacturing can adapt almost any product to sportsmen's needs. I liked it so well that I also bought a light spinning rod in the same Eagle Claw Trailmaster four-piece construction. Both rods are steady companions on wilderness trips and I am pleased to recommend them without qualification.

Let's learn the principal parts of the Trailmaster fly rod shown here. On the *cork grip* is a *locking reel seat*. The rod is joined by a *female ferrule* on the *lower section* and by a *male ferrule* on the *upper or tip section*. Just forward of the grip is a *keeper ring* to hold the hook. The line passes through six *line guides* and a *tip top*, which is the tip end of the rod. The guides are held in place by varnished *windings* of thread, and the rod itself is made of *glass cloth* specially molded into rod sections.

A 7½- or 8-foot rod should cast well with a level line whose weight size is number 6—or size "C," as it used to be called. However, if we can borrow other sizes to try on the new rod, let's also try number 5 ("D") and number 7 ("B") to see which brings out the best action.

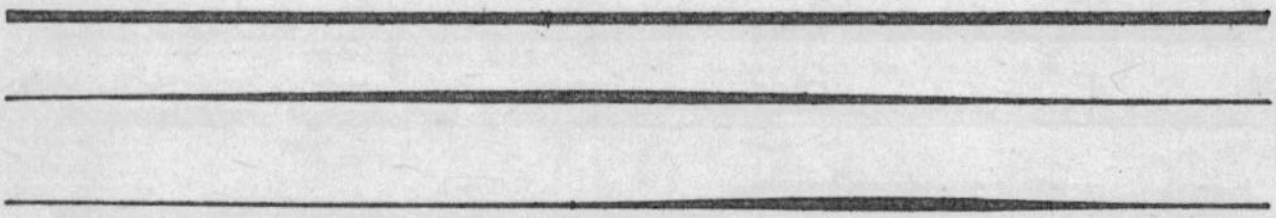

FIGURE 40
TYPES OF FLY LINES
This exaggerated drawing shows (top) a "level" line; (middle) a "double-tapered" line; and (bottom) a "torpedo-tapered" or "weight forward" line. (Forward ends are to the right.)

It may be helpful to indulge in a bit of history here to clear up confusion about fly line sizes. Fly lines used to be almost exclusively braided of silk and, all being of the same material, their sizes could be identified by letters, such as "C" for a level line; "HCH" for a double taper, and "HCF" for a torpedo (or forward) taper—these three types all being of the same basic "C" size and weight. But in 1958 we couldn't depend upon lettered sizes any more because lines also were being made of Dacron and nylon. These two are man-made materials which will not rot and become weak, as silk lines did. Thus they are more practical. But silk, Dacron and nylon each weighed differently and thus cast differently even if they were of the same diameter or size.

So, to get a standard to go by, the old lettered sizes (which went by diameter) became obsolete, and lines were identified by weight—with numbers to identify the weights. Thus, line size number 6, for example, has the same weight and fits the same rods regardless of the weight or type of material from which it is made. Some people still go by the old lettered sizes, so they are included here for comparison.

Choosing a line is made easier when the rod manufacturer recommends the proper size of line to go with it. Most of them do, now. If not, the dealer's advice may be good, but it isn't always. Anyway, it's fun to try the recommended size and also to borrow the next lighter and heavier sizes, and to try all three. A beginner should ask an experienced fly caster to check the decision.

So let's say, for example, that you are a young person in your teens who has bought a 7½-foot fly rod and is considering a size number 6 ("C") line to go with it. Here we must make a decision which hits the pocketbook. Should it be a very inexpensive level line, or a more expensive double tapered line? The double taper, as drawing 40 shows, has its designated weight in the middle, but is tapered toward both ends. This gives a double tapered line less air resistance, for longer casts, and provides less "slap" on the water, for quieter casting. If we want to fish with flies and can afford a double taper, it is a good investment. If we plan to fish with bait or other light lures, the double tapered line makes much less difference.

But we can get double tapered lines that float and others that sink. Which to choose? If we want to fish floating (dry) flies or other lures in shallow water, a floating line is necessary. If we plan to fish deep most of the time, we should have a sinking line. (A double tapered floating line in size number 6 is identified as "DT-6-F," where "DT" means "Double Taper" and "F" means "floating." In a sinking line, this would be called "DT-6-S.")

There is still another choice, and I hope you're not getting confused because I have to mention it. In addition to level lines and double-taper lines, we have "torpedo-taper" lines, where the heavy part is forward, as drawing 40 shows (with a shorter taper at the forward end). This weight-forward design provides more weight in the castable part of the line and thus contributes to longer and easier casts. It is helpful when using bass bugs, large streamer flies and bucktails, and other lures having considerable wind resistance. In the above size it would be identified as "WF-6-F" for a "Weight Forward, Floating" line. This is a rather specialized line and, for the first fishing outfit, usually the double tapered line would be more generally useful.

In summary, here is a chart of line sizes for rods of the most popular lengths:

ROD LENGTH (Medium Action)	LINE SIZE
6½ Ft.	5 or 6
7 Ft.	5 or 6
7½ Ft.	5 to 7
8 Ft.	6 or 7
8½ Ft.	7

The old line identifications for these line sizes are:

LINE SIZE	LEVEL	DOUBLE TAPER	TORPEDO TAPER
5	D	HDH	HDG
6	C	HCH	HCF
7	B	GBG	GBF
8	A	GAG	GAF

The new line identifications for these line sizes are:

LINE SIZE	LEVEL	DOUBLE TAPER	TORPEDO TAPER
5	L-5-S	DT-5-S	WF-5-S
6	L-6-S	DT-6-S	WF-6-S
7	L-7-S	DT-7-S	WF-7-S
8	L-8-S	DT-8-S	WF-8-S

(The "S" means a sinking line. For a floating line, change the "S" to "F.")

In choosing a fly line, remember again to be skeptical of "bargains" and unknown brands. It is good insurance to pay a little more, if necessary, for famous names such as Cortland, Gladding, Ashaway and Scientific Anglers —among several others.

Fly lines need care. Avoid dragging them across sharp rocks, stepping on them or doing other things that might damage the finish. Avoid storing them on the reel when wet. Pull off the wet or damp section and let it rest in loose coils until dry. Rub the line occasionally with a little line dressing on a bit of cloth to remove dirt and slime. At the end of the season, store fly lines in a cool,

FIGURE 41
TWO TYPES OF FLY REELS
(Left) a typical single action fly reel and (right) an automatic fly reel

dark place—preferably by coiling them loosely and hanging them in a plastic bag. With care, a good fly line will last for many years.

If rigid economy is necessary in choosing the first fly fishing outfit, it is better to buy a high-quality rod and line and to economize on the reel. When small and average sized fish are concerned, the quality of the reel makes little difference, because its main job is to store line and allow it to be stripped off when needed. A single-action reel of average size (between 3½ and 5 ounces, with a reel spool of 3 to 3½ inches) should fit the tackle being discussed. Here we can look for a bargain and consider low price more seriously. A typical fly reel is shown in drawing 41.

The automatic fly reel also is very popular because it takes the work out of reeling. This type winds up by means of a clock-type spring when line is stripped off. To recover line, all one has to do is to trip the lever (shown in drawing 41) by depressing it with a finger of the rod hand. This makes the spring quietly and smoothly reel in the slack and keeps the line tight whether or not a fish is taking line from the reel.

Let's assume now that we have selected a rod, reel and line, and that we want to learn how to cast with them. Let's try practice casting first, either over water or on a lawn. We won't bother with a leader and a fly or other lure for this practice session.

THE OVERHEAD CAST

Let's learn two simple but essential casts, the Overhead Cast and the Roll Cast. Others are of lesser importance and we don't need them, at least to start with.

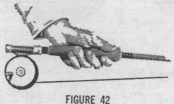

FIGURE 42
HOW TO HOLD A FLY ROD

Fly casters have several favorite ways of holding the rod, but let's begin by putting the thumb on top of the grip, pointing down the rod. Hold the rod lightly between the thumb and the lower three fingers. The forefinger remains loose, because we'll use this for other purposes.

Pull enough line from the reel so it extends from the rod tip to about double the length of the rod—about fifteen feet or so. Keep the wrist rigid, so all the action will be by bending the forearm at the elbow, with the upper arm stationary beside the body. (Later we'll use the upper arm sometimes, but let's learn without it now.) Remember that the Overhead Cast merely consists of raising the forearm upward to the vertical in an accelerating motion; pausing a second or so (longer when you have more line out), and then pushing the rod forward with another accelerating motion. Try it a few times.

While practicing, notice that when the forearm is raised the line lifts high into the air and travels backward to its full length. The forward part of the cast should start the second that the line is extended backward, so it won't have time to fall. If enough acceleration is put into the forward part of the cast, the line will shoot out straight ahead. You are casting toward a target, but you want the line to stop in the air just over the water and drop the remaining few feet to the water without slapping it—so make believe that the target is a few feet above where it is, and aim for this spot.

The Overhead Cast is mainly a matter of timing, or rhythm. You'll learn the rhythm by this practice casting. While learning, glance over your shoulder during the back cast to be sure the line is fully extended backward before starting the forward cast.

Practice this until the line lays out straight every time. Then pull a little more line off the reel and continue practicing to reach this longer distance. But don't try to handle more line than can be laid out straight.

Now, could we be doing anything wrong? The upward motion should throw the line backward, high in the air. If it drops behind you, you either are not starting the forward part of the cast soon enough, are not raising your arm smartly enough, or are flexing your wrist—which should remain rigid.

Since we are not yet trying to shoot out extra line, hold the line (just above the reel) by pressure of the forefinger against the rod grip to prevent extra line from pulling off the reel.

Note that your forearm acts as an extension of the rod,

FIGURE 43
THE OVERHEAD CAST
(Part 1: The Back Cast)

FIGURE 44
THE OVERHEAD CAST
(Part 2: The Forward Cast)

so keep rod, wrist and forearm rigid, with the elbow acting as the hinge or pivot. After a few practice casts, instinct will tell when the line has extended fully to the rear. You'll feel it by a slight tug of the rod, which will flex backward because of the pull of the line. Don't start the forward cast until the line has extended backward, but begin the forward cast the instant the line has extended.

Remember that the forward part of the cast is a smartly accelerating motion. The power of the rod and the forward acceleration you give it should extend the line straight toward the target. By aiming a few feet over the target, the line should stop over the water and then fall lightly onto it.

The combination of the backward and forward casts (which make up the Overhead Cast) becomes instinctive after a little practice. But don't try to cast more line than can be handled properly. Sloppy casting is a bad error in fishing, so cast with less line until your casts become perfect.

At this point we know enough about casting to go out and catch fish. But before putting on a leader and a fly, let's learn to cast to a greater distance. This is done by shooting out additional line.

Pull ten or fifteen feet more of line off the reel and let it drop in coils at your feet. Hold the line just below the first line guide (the butt guide) by thumb and forefinger of the hand which is not holding the rod. Cast out the line you have, making two or three practice casts. If the line is not allowed to touch the water, these are called "false casts." On one of the forward casts, let go of the line being held by the fingers just as the forward cast is being completed. Note that the speed of the line in the forward cast will pull (or "shoot") most of this extra line out also, thus extending casting distance.

To regain this extra line, reach forward with the hand not holding the rod and grasp the line just behind the butt guide. Pull this back and, holding it, reach forward again and pull back another loop. Do this until enough line has been regained to allow picking up the rest of the line by making another cast.

This extra line is held in coils by the hand not holding the rod, and coils can be transferred to the fingers for convenience. Thus, when you want to shoot out more line on another forward cast, all that is needed is to let the speed of the cast line pull off as many loops from your fingers as you wish, or as many as the power of the cast permits it to do.

There are several ways of handling this extra line, or "shooting line," as it usually is called. Practice will indicate the most comfortable way for each angler, and experienced fishermen will show you others.

Note here that we haven't said which hand should hold the rod and which one should hold the shooting line. The "rod hand" is the hand that holds the rod, and it can be whichever one is easiest. The other hand is called the "line hand." Most fishermen know how to use only one rod hand. This author has learned to use both hands equally well in casting, and has found it extremely advantageous. We can cast with one arm while resting the other. Sometimes obstructions, or the target we want to reach, make it easier to use either one hand or the other. Being able to cast with either hand also is convenient on windy days, when the hand in the direction toward which the wind is blowing should be used to keep the line from being blown toward the angler's body. It also is useful when fly fishing from a boat; one hand is handiest in casting toward the shoreline when going in one direction, the other hand when going in the other.

THE ROLL CAST

This is the second essential cast to learn, and it is best to practice it over water. It is important when obstructions are behind the caster which would make the back cast (as used in the Overhead Cast) impossible. In the Roll Cast there is no back cast.

Cast out as much line as is convenient by using a sideways cast in the easiest direction. Have some extra line off the reel to shoot out. Now, slowly raise the rod until the line extending from it is looped slightly behind and away from the shoulder of the rod hand, with the rest of the line in the water. The forward part of the cast is made by sharply pushing the rod forward and downward. When doing this, notice that the line in the water follows the loop which was extended downward behind you, and the whole line rolls out in a big loop, extending itself forward. The power of the push of the rod forward and downward will shoot out some of the extra line. How much it shoots out depends on the power of

FIGURE 45
THE ROLL CAST
(Top) The Backward Loop
(Bottom) The Forward Push

the cast, but a properly made Roll Cast will force the line out straight to a surprising distance.

One could stand only a few feet in front of a ledge or some trees or bushes and make the Roll Cast easily— which is one reason why it is important. It also is valuable in changing direction for the next cast, even if no obstructions are nearby. Make a small Roll Cast to get the end of the line on top of the water and partly to change direction. Then immediately make an Overhead Cast in any direction desired.

The Roll Cast should not be attempted until nearly all of the extended line is on or near the surface of the water, but this usually will be the case when the rod has been raised to form the loop. The Roll Cast should not be used unless necessary when water surface is calm, because it can disturb the surface enough to spoil the fishing. It works best when the surface is ripply.

LEADERS

When fishing with all fly rod lures, and especially with all types of artificial flies, a leader is a necessary connection between hook and line. Its near invisibility and length prevent fish from being alarmed by the line, and its flexibility allows the fly or lure to act as naturally as possible.

Nearly all leaders now are made from monofilament, which is the same material from which spinning and spin-casting lines are made. Various brands are stiffer or limper than others. The best leaders are made from fairly stiff monofilament, except that the sections near the fly can be more supple. All leaders should be tapered because they will cast better than level leaders and the finer end sections are more nearly invisible. Leaders average about 7½ feet in length, which is a good length for most purposes. For fishing in very clear water, leaders even as long as 14 feet, tied down to very fine tips, often are used, but beginners may find that any longer than 9 feet can be difficult to handle.

The butt of a leader (the end toward the line) should

be only slightly smaller in diameter than the thickness of the end of the line—not less than two-thirds as thick. How fine the forward end should be depends on several things: how small the fly is, the size of the fish, the clearness of the water and whether or not there are obstructions with which fish could tangle. Fishermen often make the mistake of selecting leaders whose butt diameters are too small for the line. These won't cast well. The heavy part of the leader should be about two-thirds of its length. From this it can taper down to finer diameters more quickly.

Fishermen who don't want to bother to make their own leaders can buy them cheaply. Get three or four between 7½ and 9 feet long whose butt sections are between .021 (for heavy lines) and .019 (for light lines). These will taper down to .012 or .010, and tippets between .009 and .006 can be added if necessary.

Let's skip the method of tying leaders for the present (in case you don't want to bother with it) and learn how to tie them to the line and to the fly.

Some fly lines come with small loops at the end, or fishermen can splice a loop on them. In this case, slide

FIGURE 46
THE JAMB KNOT

the leader loop up the line; thread the leader point through the line loop, and pull the two loops together tightly.

An old and easy method (sometimes most convenient, and called the "Jamb" knot) is to tie a firm knot in the end of the fly line, clipping off the excess end closely. Thread the line end through the leader loop and pass it around the loop, as drawing 46 shows. Then pass the line end under the line (over the loop). Pull the knot together at the top of the loop and work the knotted line end

closely toward the loop so there is no excess line between
the leader loop and the knot. When this is pulled together
tightly it forms a firm knot which is easy to disassemble. Many fishermen don't like this knot because it is
slightly bulky when it has to be pulled through the rod's
tip top. However, it is a very simple knot, and it is easier
to learn it from the drawing than it is to describe.

One of the smoothest and best knots for joining line
and leader is the Nail knot, which is put on without a
leader loop and which is more or less permanent. It can
be tied with a nail, but a very slender metal tube (such
as a basketball pump needle with the tip filed off) works
better. (The author likes to use the little aluminum tube
smokers often remove from pipes, if the tube is the
smooth kind.)

Here again, the drawing is easiest to follow. Hold tube

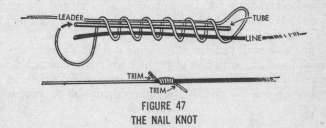

FIGURE 47
THE NAIL KNOT

and line end parallel together with the tips about even.
Lay on the end of the leader with its tip in the opposite
direction and with from 6 to 8 inches extending. Holding all three in the fingers of the left hand, wind
the leader end 6 or 7 times around itself back toward the
line end. Poke the leader end through the tube (or let
it follow back along the nail) while holding the turns together. After the leader end has been poked through,
hold the assembly in the right hand and withdraw the
tube (or nail). Pull alternately on the leader and leader
end while holding the turns tightly. When the knot has
been pulled tight, be sure to remove all slack by pulling
very tightly, first on the leader and its end and then on

both line and leader. Trim off excess line and leader ends closely, as in the sketch. Test the knot to be sure it is tight.

Chapter I shows how to tie Clinch and Turle knots, both of which are used to tie the hook to the leader.

HOW TO TIE LEADERS

When fishermen pass the beginner stage, many enjoy making some of their own lures, dressing their own flies and tying their own leaders. Sometimes this saves money, but the important point is that it is much more fun to catch fish with equipment we can make ourselves.

So, if readers want to make tapered leaders, here's how to do it. If not, go on to the next chapter and come back to the rest of this one some other time.

All we need to know to tie tapered leaders are two simple knots and a bit about how leaders should be tapered. Let's stress again that many fishermen tie (or buy) leaders tapered too lightly at the butt (line) end. These won't cast well because they won't roll the fly out properly. In fishing with bait or heavier lures, this makes little or no difference because the leader then only contributes more or less to invisibility rather than also to proper

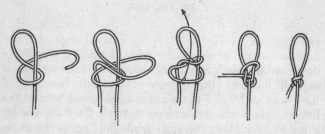

FIGURE 48
THE PERFECTION LOOP KNOT

casting—but it is valuable to know how to tie leaders correctly anyway.

We'll need to invest in several small spools of leader

material in sizes shown in Chart 52. These are not expensive, and are quite cheap when they are shared with a group. Some fishermen have decided opinions on the leader material (monofilament line) they like best. Mine is for a brand called "Blond." This golden-yellow color is highly visible in the air, making it easier to locate your fly, but it is almost invisible in the water. It has the ideal combination of stiffness and limpness both for leaders and for lines. The leader wheels on which Blond is packed are snapped together so you can carry a handy assortment of different strengths (from 2 to 30 pounds) in the pocket for streamside tying.

If we are not using the Nail knot described above, we'll want to know how to tie a strong loop on the heavy end of the leader. We should use the Perfection Loop

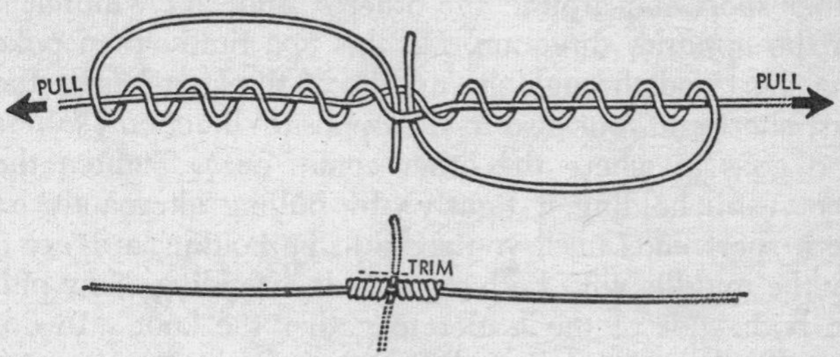

FIGURE 49
THE BLOOD KNOT

knot, and it's important to know it no matter what kind of a leader is being made.

As drawing 48 shows, hold the leader material between thumb and forefinger with several inches extending. With the other hand, make a small loop toward you and then make another loop behind the first loop with the end passing around to the front under your thumb. Now pass the free end between the two loops and, holding this firmly, work the back loop through the front loop. Work the knot tight by pulling alternately on the back loop and on the leader. When the knot has been gathered tightly you can release your fingers. The knot will look as in the drawing, with the excess end sticking out at a right angle to the leader. Trim off the excess end closely and the Perfection Loop knot is made.

The second knot is called the Blood knot or, incorrectly, the Barrel knot. It is used to tie the various lengths of monofilament together to make tapered leaders. It also is used to join two lengths of monofilament, such as when mending a broken spinning or spincasting line.

Cross the two pieces of monofilament between thumb and forefinger with several inches of both extending. Twist one of the ends around the other piece *five* times and then put the end between the fork formed by the two strands. Shift the knot to the other thumb and forefinger, holding it together in position. Now twist the other short end around the other strand, but winding it in the *opposite* direction. Do this *five* times; then poke the short end through the middle of the knot beside the first short end, but also in the opposite direction (so one end goes in where the other comes out). Tighten the knot (still holding it tightly) by pulling alternately on both short ends until you seem to be holding a figure 8 by the middle, with both short ends extending. Now pull on both ends of the leader to gather the knot. (In doing this, be careful that the short ends don't pull out.) Pull the two pieces of leader tightly and the knot will gather in even, tight coils. Snip off the short ends closely, and the knot is done.

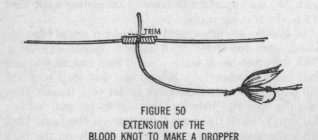

FIGURE 50
EXTENSION OF THE
BLOOD KNOT TO MAKE A DROPPER

Many people are "all thumbs" when tying this knot. If you have trouble with it, don't give up! After a bit of practice it can be done easily and quickly, and a strong Blood knot will result every time.

In gathering this knot, don't waste too much of the short ends. After pulling the knot partly tight (so the short ends won't work loose) you can push the short ends back into the knot before finally pulling it tight, so no more than an inch of each short end is wasted.

If you wish to make a dropper on your leader for tying on an additional fly or hook, it can be made at any one of the Blood knots. Merely leave one of the short ends ten inches or so long and don't cut it off after the knot is tied. This is shown in drawing 50, and it provides a very handy connection for fastening additional flies or hooks to the leader. A loop can be made on the end of this dropper by tying its end with a Perfection Loop knot.

Now that we know these two knots, we can use them to make any strength or length of tapered leader needed, and we can extend the leader at either end to fit it to a larger line or to tie on tippets. Chart 52 shows four typi-

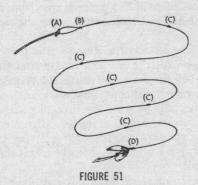

FIGURE 51
TERMINAL TACKLE KNOTS

(a) Jamb knot (or Nail knot)
(b) Perfection Loop knot
(c) Blood knot
(d) Turle knot (or Double Clinch knot)

cal leaders, of which the 7½-foot one might be good to start with. Try making this for practice, and then make some of the others when there is need for them.

While the tapered leader formulas need not be followed exactly, let's remember that the butt end should be only slightly smaller (no less than two-thirds) than the end of the line. Also, we should repeat that over half of the stronger end (the end toward the line) should be of thick leader material because this thickness or weight is needed to cast the fly properly. If a level leader, or one incorrectly tapered, is used we'll notice that at the end of a cast it will drop in coils instead of straightening out as it should. Fish rarely will strike at a fly on the end of a poorly made or badly cast leader. The tip end can taper more quickly to finer sizes, but they should be tapered gradually for smoothest casting and to enable strong knots to be tied.

When waters are low and clear, or when using very small flies, we may need to use the Blood knot to tie on finer tippets, such as a foot or more of two-pound test (.006). These fine tippets may seem too light, but they are stronger than they look and will catch more fish under these conditions if the water is free from roots, grass and other obstacles which could cause the fish to break them.

When coiling leaders for storage, it is helpful to label the envelope with the leader's length and the strength or diameter of the butt and tip ends. A micrometer is handy in testing the diameters of various sizes of leader material, especially because the strengths offered by various manufacturers vary in diameter. Micrometers are expensive, but sporting goods stores sell very inexpensive thickness gauges for lines and leaders, and these will do almost as well.

A two-inch square of inner tube rubber is handy to smooth out the coils in leaders. Hold the doubled rubber between the fingers and pull the leader between it under enough pressure to remove any kinks and coils which might develop.

| DIAMETER | .020 | .018 | .016 | .014 | .012 | .010 | .008 | .006 |
LBS. TEST	25	20	15	12	8	6	4	2
				INCHES				
7½ Ft. For								
General Use	18	18	18	12	10	8	6	
9 Ft. For Trout	24	18	18	18	12	8	10	
8 Ft. For Streamer								
Flies and Bucktails	24	18	18	12	12	12		
8 Ft. For Bass	24	24	20	18	14			

NOTE

These leaders are for line sizes 5 or smaller. For line sizes 6 or larger, add a butt section of 0.22 (30 lbs.) between one and two feet long.

For tippets of smaller leader material, add to the tip section between 12 and 18 inches of the next smaller size. If the fly does not lay out properly, cut the tippet back a little to make it shorter. All adjustments for fly size or conditions of wind and water are made with tippets.

CHART 52

SECTION LENGTHS AND SIZES FOR TAPERED LEADERS

Now that we know how to put our fly tackle together, let's see how and where to catch a few of the different kinds of fish we have in typical ponds, lakes and streams.

CHAPTER VI

STREAM FISHING

Back in my early Scouting days a leader often took me to Little River to catch trout. The first thing he'd do was to sit by the stream to study it. He always wanted to figure things out before he started fishing.

"Trout don't live everywhere in this stream," he'd say. "So why waste time fishing where they aren't? Remember that fish are a lot more like people than people might think. They like protection, so they live under undercut banks, or in the shade of stumps, logs and rocks. They don't like to battle the current, so they rest above or behind boulders in the stream where the current is much less swift. They want food, so they hide in such protective spots which are near where the main current flows and brings food down to them. If the water is too warm they try to find places where it is more comfortable, like spring holes and the mouths of brooks where cool water flows in. If the water is too cold, they go down deep where it is warmer, or they go somewhere else. Now, today, if you were a trout, where would you like to be?"

"I guess maybe I'd be close to that big stump that fell from the bank into the water," I replied after looking at the stream with new understanding. "The main current flows right by it. You can tell by the eddies between the fast water and the bank."

"Good spot," the leader agreed. "So why don't you put a lively worm on your hook the way I've told you to, and sneak quietly down to that patch of goldenrod above the stump? When you cast the worm, have plenty of slack line ready because you want the worm to drift naturally at the same speed as the current. Let the worm drift as far under the stump as you can. Try it two or three times. If you don't get a hit, remove the worm and try one of those green caterpillars we see on the bushes.

"Remember," he added as I baited my hook, "drift the worm or caterpillar *naturally*. If you hold it steady in the current, or pull it upstream, don't expect a trout to take it. Worms and caterpillars can't swim that way, you know —and trout know it, too!"

I did as he said, and caught a nice trout under the stump. Then I put on another caterpillar and caught a second fish.

Meanwhile, my friend was fishing a small streamer fly around two rocks in midstream. When I came back I watched him. He cast quartering downstream so the current would take the fly across the upstream side of the rock. On the next cast he let out more line and worked the fly on the downstream side of the rock. By twitching the rod tip, he made the fly dart around in the current exactly as if it were a live minnow. He caught a trout on the upstream side of one rock and another on the downstream side of the other. Then, seeing me watching him, he waded back.

"Why do you think these trout were lying above and below the rocks?" he asked.

"Well, maybe there's protection for them," I guessed.

"Perhaps, but when the current reaches a rock it has to split and go on both sides of it," he said. "Where it splits to go around the rock and where it joins again below the rock it leaves cones of fairly calm water. So trout can rest in these places without having to swim very hard. They can scoot under the edges of the rock if they become frightened. But if nothing bothers them, the quiet spots just above and below the rocks are good places to be when they are looking for food being washed downstream. I guess the trout thought my little streamer

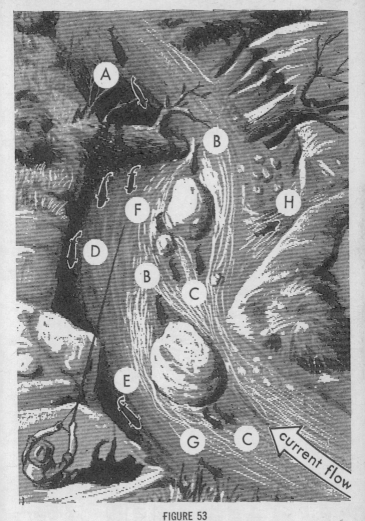

FIGURE 53
WHERE TO FIND TROUT IN STREAMS

A. Pool below fallen log
B. Below rock
C. Above rock
D. Under undercut bank

E. In deep side of bend
F. Above fallen log
G. In deep riffle
H. In mouth of feeder stream

fly was an injured minnow. I tried to fish it that way. Anyway, they took it."

We walked downstream to where a brook flowed in. "Let's sit here a moment," my instructor said. "What do you see across the river?"

I looked for a deer or some other animal, but all I saw were bushes. "Nothing," I replied.

"Look again at that very green spot on the bank. You'll see water dripping down. That's a spring hole where

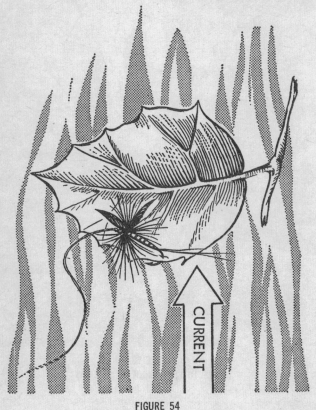

FIGURE 54
METHOD OF HOOKING A FLY TO A LEAF TO FLOAT IT
DOWNSTREAM IN BRUSHY AREA

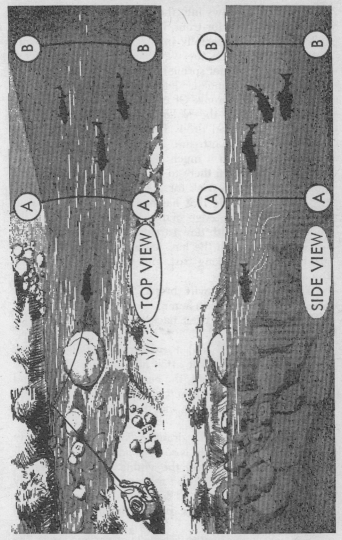

FIGURE 55
LOCATIONS OF FISH IN STREAM MOUTHS

very cold water flows into the warmer river. When river water is too warm for trout, they'll collect around spring holes like that. Especially in the summer. I'll bet you'll get a trout there on the way back. When the water is warm, always look for spring holes!

"Now," he continued, "let's decide where we might find trout in this brook. Of course they should be up in the brook because the water is cool; they have lots of protection, and food drops from bushes into the water and also drifts downstream. But it's a very bushy place, so people don't fish it much. That's the kind of place to look for. No room in there to make a back cast, or even a Roll Cast. Here's a trick for a spot like that. Cut about two inches of a twig that has one leaf on it. Hook your fly or bait into the edge of the leaf and drop it in the current. Let it drift downstream until it's where you want it; then twitch the lure loose from the leaf. Just as good as making a long cast, and you haven't disturbed the water!

"This is a fairly swift brook," he continued. "How would you fish its mouth here?"

"There might be a trout back of that rock in the middle," I guessed.

"Maybe," he said, "and it's worth a try. But the brook washes down lots of silt after heavy rains. Where the brook mouth spreads out, the current becomes slack and the silt drops to the bottom. Usually there's a steep drop-off just beyond where the mouth widens. I'll draw you a sketch of it."

He drew a sketch like drawing 55. "This isn't always so," he said, "but it often is so in ponds and lakes as well as in streams. People fish the visible part of the brook mouth when they should be fishing farther out. Usually there's a dropoff there, and fish lie in the deeper water where they have coolness, protection, and food always coming down to them.

"Now you know how to fish baits of various kinds," he went on. "Fish them naturally, letting out enough slack line to let them drift naturally. Fish often take small baits quickly and hook themselves. If you feel a hit, give the lure a very light twitch. If the fish isn't hooked, the light twitch won't move the lure very far, and the fish may come back for it. With bigger baits like nightcrawlers and minnows, don't strike too soon. Give the fish time to swallow them.

"But it's time you learned to use artificial lures a lot more and to fish natural baits a lot less," he added. "It's more fun, and often more productive, to use artificials. I've shown you how to fish streamers and bucktails. Select small ones, unless you're fishing cloudy water or big streams where there are big fish. Use dull ones on bright days and brighter ones on dull days or when the water is roily. Select ones that look like the bait fish in the water. Fish them actively with short, sharp jerks—the way a bait fish swims. Streamer flies and bucktails always are good because they imitate bait fish, and big fish eat bait fish all year round.

"Another good type of artificial is a nymph. I've told you about them. There's a lot to learn about nymph fishing, and you should read books about it. But almost any nymph often takes fish, so try this one. Notice that it's on the end of a long, finely tapered leader. That's part of the secret. Cast it out below the rock and let it drift downstream at the same speed as the current. But don't have any extra slack in the line, because fish take nymphs delicately, and you'll have to strike at the slightest suggestion of a hit. Let the nymph drift down over the dropoff. There should be some trout there."

I did as he suggested, watching the nymph wash downstream and letting out enough line so it would drift freely with the current. When the stream washed it over the dropoff I felt a slight tug, and struck lightly. I was fast to a beautiful trout, which I carefully worked toward the bank. I caught three there and decided that artificial lures really were better than bait; easier to use and a lot more fun.

"Wait a minute," the Scout leader called, as I was landing my third fish. "Let's not kill that one. We have six already. Let's let that one go so someone else can have the fun of catching him. Remove the hook carefully so he won't be hurt. Fish don't take artificial lures down deep as they often do with bait. Usually they're hooked only in the lip, so it's easy to let them go. Remember," he added, grinning, "that we're trying to teach all you fellows about conservation. In fishing, this means fishing for fun with, maybe, less than your limit to take home. The opposite of conservation is being a fish hog!"

So I let the trout go and walked back with the other two. My instructor had a little fire burning on the gravel and was cleaning two trout for lunch. A jelly glass he had found somewhere was half full of water, on a rock beside him.

"What are you doing now?" I asked.

"Seeing what this little critter had for lunch. How about a lesson in nature study—okay? Now watch! This is the trout's stomach. I'm going to slit it open and dump what's inside into this glass of water. There! What do you see?" he asked as he stirred the contents with a twig.

"Bugs."

"Well, you could be a little more definite. I'll poke them out, one by one, and put them on this paper. Two little black beetles. Four ants. A green caterpillar, slightly squashed. One little minnow. Six nymphs, and these look like houseflies, but bigger. What does that tell you?"

"That the trout had a pretty good lunch!" I said.

The Scout leader chuckled. "It tells me that these trout are eating caddis nymphs, mainly, and so I'm going to put on an imitation of a caddis nymph and catch some trout with it this afternoon.

"What a fish has in his stomach tells anglers what kind of flies to use," the Scout leader added. "In addition to this stuff, you may find crayfish, grasshoppers, spiders, worms and other things. All can be imitated with artificial lures. Learning about all this takes time, but it's part of the fun of fly fishing."

We had lunch of trout broiled on green sticks, plus a candy bar and an apple.

"People must fish here quite a lot," I remarked. "Look at those papers and tin cans! Why should folks spoil a pretty place like this by leaving refuse around?"

STREAMERS

Gray Ghost

Supervisor

BUCKTAILS

Brown-Yellow-White

Edson Dark Tiger

NYMPHS

Hendrickson Nymph

Caddis Worm

WET FLIES

Professor

Parmachene Belle

DRY FLIES

Ginger Quill

Adams

Bee

Caterpillar

Grasshopper

FIGURE 56
ARTIFICIAL FLIES

"Most people don't," the leader reminded. "It's done by a few careless goons who are lazy and don't know any better. What'll we do about it?"

"I'll squash and bury the cans. Can you burn the papers?"

In a few minutes the spot was cleaned up, the fire doused and the charcoal kicked into the current. Then we walked farther downstream to a pretty waterfall splashing into a deep pool.

"How would you fish this place?" my companion inquired.

"I'd drop a worm—I mean a streamer fly or a nymph —just below the falls and let it drift down."

"That's what most people do. At this time of day, late in the afternoon, trout probably are cruising over the shallow gravel at the tail of the pool. If we should fish where you suggest, we'd spoil the fishing in the whole pool, because the trout would see us. So let's fish this place from downstream, walking around it so we won't be seen. We'll fish the tail of the pool first and then fish up toward the falls. And the last thing we should do is to fish all the little places among the rocks right where the water is splashing down. Trout often are there, even if it's a tiny spot and only a few inches deep. Lastly, if we haven't had any luck so far, let's cast to the falls and let the fly wash down deep. If a stream is warm or very cold, the trout might be way down on the bottom."

Later, on the way back to the car, the leader said, "I'm going to come back and fish this pool just after the next rain. After a rain or a shower lots of food comes downstream, so fish are on the feed. Maybe I'll call you to see if you'd like to go along."

During the drive home I asked a lot of questions.

"Dry flies?" he answered. "We'll get to that and all the rest later. Dry flies provide the very best kind of fishing at times when fish will rise to them. But it takes quite a bit of know-how. Let's talk about what we've learned today. What did this trip teach you?"

"It taught me that fish aren't everywhere in a stream, and that if you study the water—learn to 'read' it, you said—you wouldn't waste time, so you'd have better luck. It taught me that bait fishing is okay but fly fishing is more fun. I learned what fish eat, and how to fish nymphs and streamers. I guess I learned quite a lot!"

"Well, you're young yet," he said, laughing. "You're a good Scout, and you'll learn more every time you go out. You're a fisherman now, and soon you'll be a real angler.

"One more tip, and it will be enough for today. We didn't have time to fish down as far as the bridge. Bridges cast shadows, so fish like to live under them. If you can wade downstream to proper casting distance, fish just above and around the stone abutments. Then fish down along them, and just behind them. You'll usually find the most fish quite close to the stonework. Bridges usually are good fishing spots.

"It was fun!" he added, as I took my tackle from his car. "Let's do it again, soon."

"Don't ask me if you don't want me," I said, "because I'll never say 'no' to a fishing trip. Thanks again. Thanks —a lot!"

I raced into the house because I couldn't wait to show my four beautiful trout to Mother and Dad and tell them how I caught them. Also, I was very hungry!

Streamcraft, or knowing how to "read" a stream, is one of the secrets of success in fishing. It is an art learned gradually, because fish live in certain places in a stream at one time of year, and in other places at other times. Areas which may be pleasantly cool for them in spring and fall may be much too warm in summer. Spawning migrations, water depth and other factors also must be considered.

Generally, though, in addition to my lesson on this early trip, we found other places where trout like to live in streams. Where two currents merge above a pool; the deeper pockets in shallow riffles flowing over rocks and gravel, and long, swift runs in eddying currents, for example. We learned that, where water is deep on one side of a stream and shallow on the other, it is best to walk or wade the shallow side and to fish toward the deep side. There, if we don't get fish on or near the surface, we should fish deeper along or close to the bottom.

Smallmouth bass inhabit rocky areas of trout streams in many regions, but usually are found in deep pockets or pools. Chub like mildly moving water and often are caught in the same places and with the same lures as are trout. Suckers inhabit lakes, ponds and the backwaters of rivers, but migrate up brooks and streams in the spring to spawn. While suckers are not considered to be game fish, they can provide real sport in spring when many small streams are filled with them.

So-called trash fish like chubs and suckers provide more fishing fun than most people think they do. What they may lack in fighting ability is more than made up for by their great numbers. There's no bag limit, so catch all you want—and serve the cause of conservation at the same time by helping to rid the streams of them.

Izaak Walton, the "patron saint" of anglers, considered fishing to be "the contemplative man's recreation." When fishing streams, it isn't wasting time to sit where there's a good view of the water and contemplate where the best fish should be in it. Thinking things over and planning how to fish a stretch of water usually results in having to make fewer casts to catch more fish!

CHAPTER VII

POND AND LAKE FISHING

During college a very special friend was a Supervisor of Game Wardens of the State of Maine—a noted angler and naturalist who delighted in passing on his knowledge to young people. We canoed into the wild country every spring and every fall, year after year. It was mainly from him that I learned the secrets of where big fighting fish are found, why they are there, and how to catch them. From him I also learned how to travel in the wilderness and how to live in the woods, plus fascinating lore about plants, animals, minerals and other secrets of nature.

"Now this," the warden once said when we were on a lake in southern Maine, "is a bass lake. Most or perhaps all are smallmouth bass, which like colder, deeper water than largemouth bass do. Largemouth bass like fairly shallow water from 60 to 80 degrees. Both kinds live where there's protection and food and, since they generally eat about the same things and are caught in about the same ways, we won't get confused right now by going into the differences between the two species.

"I remember fishing this lake as a kid," he went on. "All I had was a cane pole and some line with a leader, a bobber and a hook—usually number 6, if I remember. I learned to fasten the bobber two or three feet above the hook so the hook would ride just over the weed beds or the bottom. I'd crimp on a small split shot a few inches above the hook to keep the bait down. There was a trick to using the bobber. It should be so light it just barely floats. Then, when a fish took the bait, he couldn't feel the pull of the bobber. The bait felt more natural. Nowadays we have plastic ball floats that can be filled partly with water to give them whatever buoyancy is needed. I used to make mine from corks, and I made several sizes to suit the weights of various baits. I'd get a big long needle or something similar, hold it with pliers and heat it very hot, and burn a hole through the middle of the cork. I would push the leader or line through it, hold it in place with a matchstick or part of a toothpick inserted in the hole, and there you'd be!

"Well, I knew that bass came into the shallows to feed in the evening, so I'd row over to the lily pads or weed beds and fish such places. I used minnows, worms, crayfish, spring salamanders, hellgrammites—almost anything. I'd just toss the rig into an open spot amid the pads or grasses and wait for a bass to take the bait. Usually didn't have to wait long. Now we've got good spinning outfits and really can do business!

"While we're sitting here, let's look this lake over," the warden continued. "See those points of land with submerged grasses at their tips? We'll fish with plastic worms all around the points, from ten to twenty feet deep. In the evening we could fish nearer the surface, but at midday the bass probably are lying down deep." He pointed. "Around that stump is a good place. So is that rock ledge going into deep water. Actually, anywhere bass can find shade is worth trying—near a raft, around docks, under submerged logs and trees, off rocky bars, in shady coves —lots of places. You have to mosey around and find out where they are.

"There's one thing to remember," he went on. "Bass often come into shallow water in the early morning and in the evening for food. Sometimes you can hear and see them splashing, so you know where to cast. But when the sun is high it's better to try for them in deep water. It's late morning, so let's fish deep around the points."

We started the little Johnson motor on the skiff and

went to the nearest point, anchoring the boat off and to one side of it.

"Some people like these plastic worms and some

FIGURE 57
FISHING DEEP WATER OFF A POINT OF LAND

don't," the warden said. "I love 'em, but you have to fish 'em right. You can use the floating kind and fish 'em like a little eel, swimming, but here we'll have to put a lead jig on and fish them deep. Cast out and let the worm sink. Imagine it with its head on the bottom and its tail waving up in the water. Now reel very, very slowly and keep a tight line. Make the worm crawl very slowly toward you, stopping it every once in a while. No! That's too fast. *Very* slowly, I said."

I cast again.

"If you feel anything—anything at all that doesn't feel natural—drop your rod tip a second or two, and then strike. If it's a bass, you'll know it!"

Following his instructions, I made several casts in a semicircle nearby. Then I lengthened the casts and cast fanwise several times again, as drawing 57 shows. Finally I had cast in several arcs, the last one as far as I could reach. Then we moved to the other side of the point to finish fishing the area thoroughly. We caught three bass, but I became snagged once and had to break loose. We spent an hour at the spot and then tried others.

"I should think you'd lose a lot of lures this way," I said.

"You'll lose one occasionally, especially when fishing around stumps and submerged trees, but that's where the bass are. Usually, with this ten-pound test line, you can pull 'em loose. If it's too weedy or brushy, use a weedless hook."

That evening we drifted the boat around masses of lily pads and tried other casting lures with spinning tackle. We started with popping plugs.

"You're fishing your plug too fast," the warden said. "Imagine how a frog acts when he jumps off a lily pad. He often just sits in the water for as long as a minute or two. Then he may swim a bit and rest again. Fish your popper that way. Let it rest on the water until after the ripples stop. Then give it a very light jerk to make it pop the water slightly. Rest it again and continue the same way until you have fished out your cast. Be methodical and fish slowly. Cover all the good spots, one at a time, casting in an arc either to the right or to the left."

I followed instructions, and on the second cast there was a heavy splash and the plug disappeared. It was a big pickerel which put up a good fight. Later a bass hit the lure, jumped several times, and tangled around a lily pad stem. I worked him loose and put him on the stringer.

"Now let's try a floating-diving plug and fish the deeper water away from the pads," the warden suggested.

"What color?" I asked.

"Color is less important than the kind of action the plug has and the way you fish it. Here's one with a dark back and a light belly. It looks like a small bluegill. Try it."

I put it on and cast it out, letting the plug float a short time before fishing it in.

"A slow, steady retrieve is a good way to fish a floating-diving plug," the warden commented. "When you start to fish it in, the lip on the front pulls it under the water. The faster you fish it the deeper it goes. Now suppose you are fishing along a ledge where the water is very deep, during a condition when surface water is too warm or during midday when bass are near the bottom. You could use a sinking plug under such conditions. You cast it out and let it sink, counting the seconds. If you don't get a strike on the retrieve, or if it doesn't touch bottom, allow another second or two for it to sink deeper. The idea is to fish it in just over the bottom. If you feel it touch bottom, reel a little faster to make it go less deep.

"A good plug caster isn't made in a day," the warden added. "Watch successful fishermen. Try the lures they use and fish 'em the way they do. What's good one day may be no good the next, so you have to experiment. You learn and you remember past experiences. After a while you get the hang of it and can pretty well guess what lure to select and how to fish it for any condition."

While I experimented, the warden laid down his spinning rod and picked up a fly rod with a tiny cork-bodied popping bug on the leader. He made a false cast and dropped the bug in a "V" in the lily pads. After resting it a minute he popped it a few times, slowly and delicately. A four-pound bass splashed up and took it.

"This little lure also is one of my pets for bluegills," the warden said as he put the bass on the stringer. "When the sun isn't out, bluegills will feed on the sur-

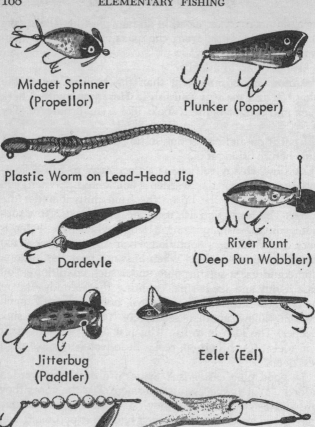

Midget Spinner
(Propellor)

Plunker (Popper)

Plastic Worm on Lead-Head Jig

Dardevle

River Runt
(Deep Run Wobbler)

Jitterbug
(Paddler)

Eelet (Eel)

C.P. Swing (Spinner)

Pork Rind

Pikie Minnow (Floating-Diving)

FIGURE 58
CASTING LURES FOR BASS AND OTHER BIG POND FISH

face. Often you can see them splashing and swirling near the pads. Then little cork popping bugs or deer-hair bugs work very well. But when the sun is out bluegills usually won't feed on top. Then, with a fly rod, try little trout streamers or bucktails on number 10 or 12 hooks, or

Cork Bodied Popper   Bass Bug

Deer Hair Bug   Bee   Bivisible Dry Fly

Wulff Dry Fly   Splay-Wing Streamer   Jig

Flatfish   Red & White Wobbler

FIGURE 59
FLY ROD LURES FOR LARGE AND SMALL POND FISH

sponge-bodied bugs with legs made of small rubber bands. Sink them and fish them in slowly, with small twitches of the rod tip. If you get no strikes, try it a little deeper. Bluegills are a member of the sunfish family. They are called 'bream' in some places. These little critters have small mouths, so you should use small lures—

almost any kind of worm or insect, or the little jigs or artificial flies which imitate them."

"At camp in the summer," I said, "we used to fish for yellow perch, but we didn't catch very many."

"Perch will hit a great variety of lures any time of the year regardless of time of day or of the weather," the warden commented. "They are tough little fighters on light tackle, and a real treat to eat. You'll find them where you find bass and bluegills; also out in shallow ponds and lakes where there are patches of weed beds on clean, sandy bottom. Perch are great worm stealers, and are more cautious and slow in striking than bluegills are. The best live bait are small minnows, but they'll eat almost anything. They'll really grab a minnow, but you have to give a perch a second or two to turn it in his mouth because he swallows it head first. Don't wait more than a second or two, or he'll strip your hook. After you've caught a few you'll get the hang of it.

"In fishing with minnows for perch," the warden went on, "the bobber method we talked about works well. Perch travel in schools and you have to locate the schools. So troll the bobber very slowly, rowing the boat over or near weedy patches until you catch a good fish. Then anchor and fish there. When you find a school of big perch you can use light spinning or spin-casting tackle, or a fly rod. Perch rarely take surface lures, so fish deeper, just over the weed beds. Small spinners, spoons and jigs work well. But the perch will try to take your lure down into the weeds, so watch out for that!

"And speaking of jigs, here's an idea for a jig you can make quickly, plus a way to keep perch from stealing worms. Pinch a split shot on the shank of the hook just back of the eye. Paint it red with finger nail polish, if you wish. Then cover the rest of the hook with half a worm. Of course you have to give this lure action by jigging it—that is, by twitching it up and down lightly. It's a good way to catch most kinds of small pond fish."

Another year, late in the spring, the warden invited me to meet him at his place on a little lake in Maine. He had a small aircraft waiting, resting on its pontoons beside

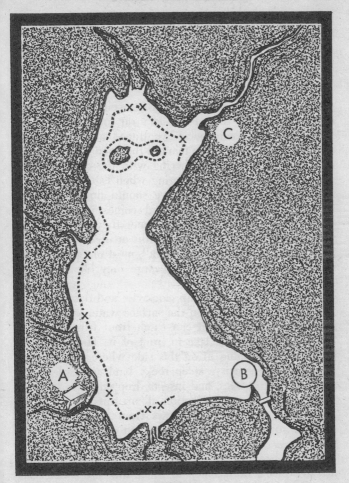

FIGURE 60

TROLLING AND CASTING SPOTS ON A TYPICAL TROUT LAKE

(a) Our camp   x = Brook mouths
(b) Outlet and dam   - = Path of good trolling
(c) Inlet stream

the dock. We flew to an isolated lake in northern Maine and stayed in an abandoned lumber camp. The old log cabin had been used by squirrels and mice all winter and there were signs that a bear had broken in. But we swept out the place and patched it up and made it quite comfortable.

"This week," the warden said that evening as we sat on a log in front of the cabin, "let's do some trolling. To show you the good spots, I've traced a topographical map of this lake, and I've marked the good fishing places on it. There's no use bothering with the others except perhaps in the very early spring when fish might be almost anywhere. Right now we should find them near the brook mouths because food comes into the lake there. When the water gets warmer they'll be in deep water, close in by the brook mouths or up in the brooks. Since these trout spawn in the fall, most of them will be up in the brooks then, too, because they like to spawn in gravelly brooks.

"Let's go around the map clockwise and decide where we should fish now, when the surface water is cool. Our camp is at 'A,' and you can catch trout from shore in the brook and in the lake in front of it. There are two more brooks coming in on this side where I've marked 'x.' Between them is a steep rocky bank with plenty of shade from the trees, and insects dropping into the water. Good food and protection all up this side. Also, in good weather the breeze blows from west to east, or from 'C' to 'A.' This drifts insects and other food to this side.

"At the head of the lake are two islands, with a shallow gravel bar between them. Since they are rocky, fishing should be good around them. At the head of the lake it's very swampy, and a brook splits and flows in there. There's a steep dropoff about twenty-five feet from shore, so it's a good place to anchor for fly fishing or spinning. A big stream comes in at 'C,' so fishing all around the head of the lake should be good. But there's not much reason for fish to be from 'C' down to 'B,' and it is very shallow and rocky in the cove. The cove is full of chubs; you can have some fun with them if you want to. At the head of the cove is an old log dam, with a small pool below it and a big pool farther down. Fishing is only fair in the pools now, but it's excellent in the fall when trout are running upstream. Lastly, at the bottom of the sketch you'll see where two brooks come in. You can see the place off to your right, but the brooks are hidden in grass and small bushes. It's very swampy, and moose often feed there.

"So now you know why all the spots marked 'x' should have good fishing. Sneak up on them quietly. Anchor well off or to one side of the brook mouths. Let the anchor down carefully and make no noise in the boat. Cast carefully so your line will disturb the water as little as possible. If you're using a wet fly or streamer, fish it near the surface for a few casts. If you get no strikes, try letting a few casts go down deep. If no results then, change the fly. This lake has a lot of small smelt in it. Now they're about two inches long. So try a streamer of the same size that imitates a smelt—my 'Supervisor,' or a 'Gray Ghost' or a 'Ballou Special,' for example. I'll be away all day tomorrow, so you can go out and fool around a bit. Save two or three big trout for dinner, but don't kill more than we can eat. If the fishing is as good as it should be, pinch the barb off the lucky fly. With a barbless hook you can land the fish on a tight line, or can let them shake loose by giving them some slack.

"Now," the warden went on, "let's talk about trolling. You should troll a streamer or bucktail, or a minnow and most other lures, fairly fast; about five miles an hour, or as fast as a man can walk. With the water as cool as it is, try trolling close to shore. I've marked the best places with this dotted line on the map. Follow the shoreline, going into all the little coves. If you don't get strikes near the surface, troll out a little farther and fish a little deeper.

"Later in the year," the warden added, "the surface water will be too warm for trout, except in spring holes and perhaps around stream mouths. Warm water is lighter than cold water, so it stays in a layer on top. This warm layer may be ten feet deep or so. Under that, the water gets colder rapidly. That's why you usually should troll deep in summer, even if you have to use a wire line or something similar."

While the warden was away I explored the lake, casting around the stream mouths and trolling where he had recommended. Most of the trout were about ten inches long, brilliantly speckled with dark backs and orange-pink shaded to white underneath. They were wild trout,

FIGURE 61
"MENDING" THE LINE

boring to the bottom when hooked, swirling to the surface and providing far more action than one ever gets with stocked fish. They liked a small black, green and white bucktail so well that I pinched down the barb and played with them, letting every one go except for two big trout which we wanted for dinner.

In the afternoon I tried the far shore, but the fishing was as poor as the warden had predicted. When the sun had set, a hatch of large flies emerged, skimming and dipping over the water. Fishing the brook mouth at camp with a dry fly seemed inviting, so I went home and put a floating line and a finely tapered leader on my favorite Eagle Claw glass fly rod. The warden's dry fly box was handy and contained a fly similar to the hatch that now had become swarms of flying insects.

Deciding to try the tackle before fishing the stream mouth, I made a cast off shore. The leader floated and had a few coils in it, but rubbing it with mud and stretching it made it straight and caused it to sink as it should. A cast over the stream mouth dropped the fly lightly in the current, where it floated naturally until the current caught the line, thus making the fly start to swing and drag. A dry fly being pulled against the current usually won't take fish, but "mending the line" is the remedy for this. With the line on or near the surface, all one has to do is to flip the rod tip in the opposite direction to that in which the current is curving the line. This reverses, or partly reverses, the curve, thus allowing the fly to drift again in a normal manner for a short time. When the fly starts to drag again, and the line can't be mended, it is time to pick up the fly for another cast.

Shadows cast by the hills were deepening on the lake when the warden returned down the old logging road. "I've been watching you," he greeted, "and the fishing seems to be good. Glad to see you're using a floating fly. Dry flies provide the most exciting kind of fishing. I guess I'll get my rod and join you. I love to see a trout slurp up and grab a fly off the surface. What are you using?"

"One of your dry flies," I said. "It seemed to match the hatch pretty well. What kind of a hatch is it?"

"Green Drakes," the warden said. "Up here they hatch every year about now. Trout love them! Some day I'll show you how to catch trout by 'dapping' with them."

The week passed too quickly. On Saturday the little plane flew in to take us back. That was many years ago, when aircraft were uncommon in the Maine wilderness; when waterways were the only other means of travel, and the few sportsmen who fished the wild lakes took no more trout than they needed. A cast then into a pool below an old log dam would make several big trout flash up to take the fly. Aircraft, roads and outboard motors have changed all that but, in many places, the fishing still is good. Some of the lakes still are wilderness lakes, with rarely used campgrounds unspoiled by carelessly discarded rusting cans and empty bottles.

The kindly warden is with us no more, but among the little treasures he gave me is that "Green Drake" dry fly. A small label is attached to the hook, and it rests in a tiny plastic box all by itself. I'll never use it again.

The warden always was careful about releasing fish, not because he was a warden, but because he was a sportsman. "Put the small ones back so they can grow up," he used to say. "The day will come when there will be too few of them." He rarely used a net. When fishing from shore he would lead the fish to a place where, by walking backward with a tight line, the fish would flop into shallow water or onto the beach. When freeing a fish, he would release it without touching it unless necessary. With the fish in the water, he would hold the hook by its bend and turn it so the fish could drop off. If the fish should be too exhausted to stay upright he would hold it upright with his hands delicately around its body, moving it back and forth in the water until it had breathed enough to swim away.

When wading, or fishing from a boat, he released the hook similarly. If he had to hold the fish, or wanted to land it, he grasped it with thumb and forefinger circled around the back of its neck, the tips of the thumb and forefinger pressed under its gills. This is a secure grip for average-sized fish, which temporarily paralyzes them so they can be lifted from the water without wiggling. He enjoyed showing people this trick because the fish rarely moved. But when he removed the hook and set the fish

At Water Surface Temperatures	Water Is	Fish Are	Fishing Should Be	Fish Are Found	Suggested Lures
FREEZING TO 40°F	MUCH TOO COLD	INACTIVE	VERY POOR	VERY DEEP (In lakes or pools)	BAIT FISHED DEEP
40°—50°F	TOO COLD	PASSIVE	FAIR	DEEP (Or along shorelines or riffles where winter is warmer)	LIVE BAIT, SPOONS OR SPINNERS NYMPHS STREAMER FLIES
50°—60°F	JUST RIGHT	ACTIVE	GOOD	NEAR SURFACE	WET FLIES STREAMER FLIES NYMPHS SPOONS OR SPINNERS
60°—70°F	JUST RIGHT	VERY ACTIVE	EXCELLENT	NEAR SURFACE	DRY OR WET FLIES STREAMER FLIES NYMPHS SPOONS OR SPINNERS
70°—80°F	TOO WARM°	ACTIVE TO PASSIVE°	FAIR	DEEP (Or in spring holes, brook mouths, shaded streams)	LIVE BAIT STREAMER FLIES NYMPHS SPOONS OR SPINNERS
80°F AND UP	MUCH TOO WARM	INACTIVE	VERY POOR	VERY DEEP (Or in spring holes and cold-water brooks)	BAIT FISHED DEEP

OPTIMUM TEMPERATURES

TOLERANT TEMPERATURES

°These ranges are more accurate for brook trout than for rainbow or brown trout which are active at temperatures about 5° higher than shown here.

While all anglers and scientists will not agree completely with these ranges, they are the most generally accepted. The optimum temperatures for bass are between 60° and 80°.

© 1949 and 1967 by J. D. B., Jr.

CHART 62   TEMPERATURE—ACTIVITY TABLE FOR TROUT

back into the water it always flashed away, evidently un-harmed.

He landed bass and other sharp-spined fish by hold-ing them by the lower jaw with his thumb in the mouth and his forefinger under the jaw. Sharp-toothed species like big pickerel and pike which he wanted to keep were picked up by pressing thumb and forefinger into the eye sockets. He carried a pair of "fish gripper" pliers to hold the lower jaws of those he wanted to let go, so he could release the hook. The fish he kept always were killed im-mediately, either by bending the head back far enough to break the neck, or by hitting the fish smartly on the head with a small club he called a "priest." Although fish evidently cannot feel pain, he disliked to let them flop in captivity. I never saw him waste a fish, except those of the trash varieties like chubs, carp and suckers, which he thought should not be returned to the water. The few fish he wanted for food always were killed quickly, cleaned promptly, and were kept cool and dry. Thus they were delicious when the warden cooked them in his various expert ways, and he always served them with pride.

I hope there are many young people who will grow up to be like him.

CHAPTER VIII

TYING FLIES IS FUN!

"It's time you learned to tie your own flies," the warden said one evening as we sat at a porcupine-chewed, lamplighted table in a fishing shack in the back country. "Tying flies is fun, and you'll have more sport catching fish on flies you've tied yourself. Fly tying can be a lifelong hobby just like fishing is, and of course the two go well together. Loads of people tie their own flies, from the top brass in big corporations all the way down the line.

"We never kill songbirds for their feathers," the warden continued. "Very few are suitable anyway. Most feathers used in fly tying are from barnyard fowl, some being dyed various colors. Pheasants, partridges, ducks and other game birds provide useful feathers. Other birds such as peacocks, gamecocks and several species of pheasants are raised for them. Deer tails, either natural or dyed, are used a great deal, plus the pelts of bears, squirrels, rabbits, foxes and other animals shot for game. The bodies of flies are made from wool, silk, chenille, tinsel and other materials. It's easy to collect such things gradually.

"It's simplest to learn the essentials of fly tying from a good fly tyer, rather than from books, because it's easier to show people the various simple steps than it is to describe them. But let's forget that I've brought along my fly tying kit. Let's assume you are home and all you have is a few hooks plus whatever you can find around the house or that you can come by without spending any money. The family sewing basket will provide a spool of black thread and a small pair of scissors. One of the girls will lend you her finger nail polish to lacquer parts of the fly so it will hold together. Someone who does knitting will give you a few feet of yarn of various colors, preferably black, bright yellow and red. A squirrel that crossed the road at the wrong time won't mind your taking his tail. The attic may provide discarded ladies' hats with feathers in such colors as red, white and yellow. We'll start with that, and you gradually can build

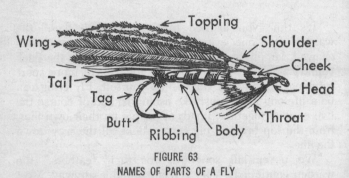

FIGURE 63
NAMES OF PARTS OF A FLY

up your kit with things you find or can swap for. There's very little you'll need to buy.

"People tie flies without a vise," the warden went on, "but a vise is handy to hold the hook. You'll want to have a vise especially made for tying flies, but any small one will do for a start. Let's begin with a simple bucktail fly with a yarn body and a squirrel tail wing. Here's a number 6 long-shanked hook with a turned-down eye—a good type to use for a bucktail. Clamp the lower part of it in the vise, tightly, like this.

"Now we'll wind the hook's shank with thread to make a base for the fly. Cut off about a yard of thread and lay the end on the shank of the hook, pointing toward its bend. Holding it there with thumb and forefinger of

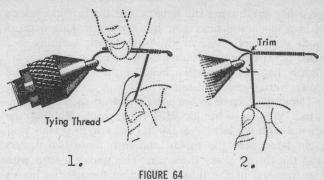

FIGURE 64
STARTING THE WINDING

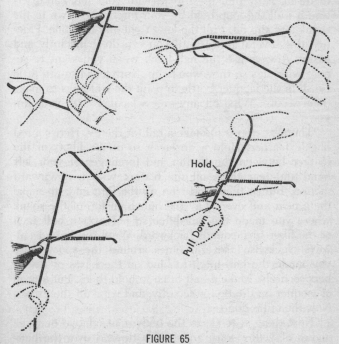

FIGURE 65
HOW TO MAKE A HALF HITCH

your left hand, wind the long part of the thread back on it in a clockwise direction. If we were making a tinsel body we would make all the turns tightly together, but with a yarn body we don't need to be so fussy. Wind tightly back to where the bend of the hook starts, and don't overlap any windings.

"Now we'll have to anchor the thread so it won't unwind. We use a simple Half-Hitch knot. Holding the thread with the left hand, lay the first two fingers of your right hand over the thread and turn these two fingers and the thread away from you. This makes a loop with the free end of the thread extending toward the hook's bend. Put this complete loop around the hook's shank, holding it with your forefinger and using another finger to press it against the shank exactly where you want it to tie in. Now pull the thread with your left hand, letting it pull the loop held by your forefinger down to the shank and slip off. Pull the knot tight and it's done. Practice this several times until you can do it instantly and easily. Always use the half-hitch when you want to secure windings so they won't slip. Now let's use the little brush in the lacquer bottle to paint the windings to make them secure. Wipe off any excess lacquer with your finger.

"The next step is to make a tail for the fly. Here's a red hackle feather. Hold a dozen or so of the fibers of the feather between the thumb and forefinger of your left hand and tear them off the feather with a downward motion. Bunch them and trim off the torn ends to make them neat and even. Lay the bunch on top of the shank where you made the half-hitch so not over a half inch of the fiber tips extends backward. Wind the thread (always clockwise) several times around the spot where you made the half-hitch to bind on the bases of the fibers securely. Make a half-hitch to hold them. Put a drop of lacquer on the tie for security, and wipe off the excess. Now the tail is done.

"Next thing is to tie in the body. Cut off two or three inches of yellow yarn and hold a tip end over the half-hitch. (If we were going to include tinsel for ribbing,

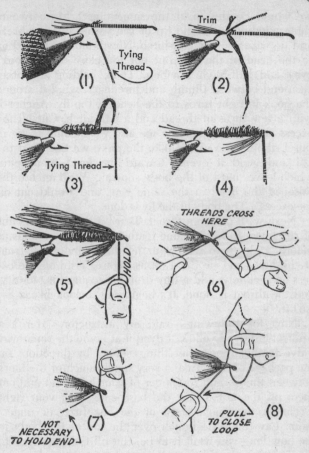

FIGURE 66

STEPS IN TYING THE FLY DESCRIBED, INCLUDING
MAKING THE WHIP FINISH

(Illustrations 1 through 5 show steps in tying a simple fly as described in
the text. Illustrations 5 through 8 show how to tie the Whip Finish, as
described in text and below:

(5) Head wound neatly, ready to make Whip Finish.

(6) Make loop, threads crossing where finish will be started.

(7) Hold thread coming from fly. Wind it around head several times to
    rear of head. (Use both hands.)

(8) Pull loop tight **around** head.

we would tie this in at the same time.) Make two or three windings over the tip of the yarn with the thread and tie with another half-hitch. Now wind the thread up to the head of the fly (but not too close to the hook's eye) and half-hitch it again. Then, holding the other yarn end between thumb and forefinger, wind it around the hook in tight turns to the head of the fly. Anchor it with a few turns of thread and a half-hitch. Cut off the excess yarn. (Now here, if we also were going to tie in tinsel ribbing, we would take the piece we tied in at the tail and wind it evenly toward the head in a spiral which leaves most of the body showing. We'd anchor the tinsel at the head in the same way, and would cut off the excess.) The body of the fly is done.

"Next, we'll put on a throat. Tear off the same amount of red fibers from the same feather and trim the ends as before. Hold them with your left hand under the front of the body and tie them on as before. Trim off the excess ends closely; add a tiny drop of lacquer for security, and the throat is done. It's beginning to look like a fly, isn't it?

"Now for the wing," said my instructor. "Here's a squirrel tail dyed yellow. I dyed it at home the same way I dye feathers and other things, going by directions on the package of dye. Take a very small bunch of the hairs between thumb and forefinger of your left hand and cut them off the tail. Brush the base ends with your right forefinger to remove most of the fine fuzz, or underhairs. Lay this little bunch over the top of the body to see how long you want it to be. Cut off the base ends to the right length and paint the extreme tips with lacquer, pressing it in and removing excess with thumb and forefinger. This insures a tight tie so the wing won't pull out later. Now lay the bunch of hairs on top of the shank so the ends come almost, but not quite, to the hook's eye. Make several turns of thread, wound on very tightly, to hold them down, and then wind the thread closely and evenly toward the eye, and perhaps back and forth a little, until the head looks neat.

"Nearly all flies are tied off at the head by a concealed

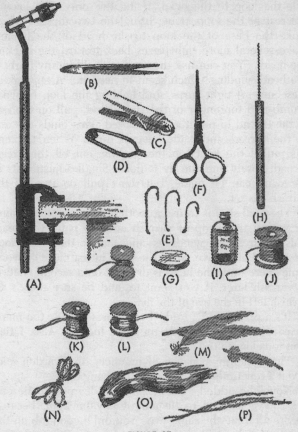

FIGURE 67
FLY-TYING EQUIPMENT

(a) Vise (b) Tweezers (c) Homemade hackle pliers (d) Professional hackle pliers (e) Hooks (f) Scissors (g) Wax (h) Bodkin needle (i) Head cement (j) Tying thread (k) and (l) Heavy and fine tinsel (m) Neck hackles (n) Wool yarn (o) Squirrel tail (p) Peacock herl

knot called a Whip Finish, and it's an easy one you must learn. Start with a loop as you did when making a half-hitch. Then hold between thumb and forefinger of your right hand the part of the thread that extends from inside the loop to the head. Using this only, and leaving the rest of the loop alone, bring the two threads which make the base of the loop to the head of the fly and make several more tight turns back toward the back of the head. (You can use these turns to fill in any parts of the head winding which seem to need it.) After making these several tight turns, and holding the loop between thumb and forefinger of the right hand, pull on the end of the thread to pull the loop closed. This binds the end of the thread under the several turns. When the end has pulled the knot together tightly, cut off the excess thread closely and the fly is done. Small adjustments in the wing can be made, but don't pull on it until the varnish has set.

"The final step is to use a toothpick or something similar with a tiny drop of varnish on it to paint the head. This secures the windings and makes the head look glossy and attractive. Stick the barb into a piece of wood somewhere until the head is dry. Put on a second coating of varnish later, if you want to, and be sure there's no varnish left in the eye of the fly."

"It's a pretty fly," I said, "but I guess I made too many turns of thread and made the head too big. Also, I tied a bit too close to the eye."

"That's merely a matter of practice," the warden said. "Do it a few times and you'll get the hang of it.

"Now," he added, "you've not only learned to tie one fly. You've learned to tie almost any bucktail, because they're all done the same way. You did a good job on the first try, and you'll probably catch some fish with that fly tomorrow. It's a good pattern for trout, bass, pickerel and lots of other fish.

"I've brought you a few little presents," he went on. "Here's a fly tying vise and spools of wide and narrow gold and silver tinsel. Another item you'll find you'll need later is a pair of hackle pliers to hold the end of your thread taut and to hold hackle tips when winding on hackles to make collars and dry flies. You can buy metal hackle pliers, but I've whittled this one for you from a spring-type wooden clothespin. To make 'em, all you need to do is to file or whittle the clamp end like this (see drawing) and wind a rubber band back of the clamp to make it tight enough. You'll also need what fly dressers call a bodkin to pick varnish out of hook eyes, to adjust hackles, and so forth. Here's one I made for you by pushing the eye end of a large needle into a wooden dowel.

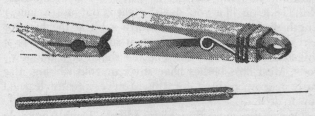

FIGURE 68
HOW TO MAKE HACKLE PLIERS FROM A CLOTHESPIN—
AND A BODKIN FROM A DOWEL AND A NEEDLE

"When you get home, get a tackle box or something similar and keep your fly tying stuff in it so you can take it on fishing trips. Then you can tie flies as you want 'em, when you want 'em, and have something to do on rainy days. Also, here's a book on fly tying. There's so much to learn about it that we can't learn it all here, but you can study how to make fancy streamers and bucktails, as well as other wet flies and dry flies and nymphs. You know enough now so the rest will be easy, and you can absorb it gradually."

I thanked the warden for his gifts and his thoughtfulness. "You said I've learned tonight to tie almost any bucktail," I said. "I'd like to make one with a silver body. How do I do it?"

"Easy!" the warden said. "When you wind the thread down the body, make the windings as close as possible, without overlapping, to provide a smooth base. Cut off a few inches of the wide tinsel and cut the end to a point so it will tie in easily. After putting on the tail, tie the tip of the tinsel in where you half-hitched the tail on and loop the tinsel over the windings to conceal them. Continue to wind the tinsel closely to the head without overlapping. You can adjust windings with your finger nail. Tie the tinsel off at the head and cut off the excess. And you'd better paint the body with lacquer so it won't tarnish.

"Silk and rayon floss make good bodies," the warden went on, "and you can get floss in every color imaginable. Tie it on like you did the yarn, but use a longer length. By winding back and forth a bit at the forward part of the body, you can shape it sort of cigarlike so it will look pretty and more like the shape of a minnow's body. Most floss bodies have silver or gold ribbing. Use fairly narrow ribbing for this. You've already learned how to do it.

"One or two more things," he added. "Double or triple wings make good bodies because you can tie in light-colored hair with a darker color over it, and perhaps a darker color over that—like black over brown over white or yellow, for example. This gives your fly more of the coloration of a bait fish. But when you tie on a double wing, use only half as much hair for each of the two layers. For a triple wing, use only a third as much. All you do is to tie one bunch on over the other. But don't use too much hair. Use less than you think you should. You want the wing to be slender, like the body of a bait fish. You don't want it to look like a brush!

"After you've learned to tie simple bucktails you can go on to fancy ones with cheeks and eyes and peacock herl topping and all that sort of thing. Then you can learn how to do streamers—the flies that also imitate minnows but whose wings are tied mostly with feathers. Tying nymphs and dry flies also takes more study and practice, but you now know the basic essentials. All this is in the book I gave you, and I hope it leads to years of fun in fly tying.

"And finally," the warden said, "let me give you a bit of advice. Learn one type of fly thoroughly before you try another type. Copy established patterns you want to fish with. Don't try to invent flies, at least at the start, because all you'll end up with is junk. Well, it's getting late. Let's go to bed and get up early so you can catch the first trout on the first fly you ever tied all by yourself."

The next day I caught the trout; several, in fact, all on that little bucktail. Needless to say, I worked at fly tying every spare moment during the trip, with the warden usually sitting nearby and offering comments and suggestions on whatever he thought was right or wrong. That was many years ago, and I've been devoted to the art ever since. Experienced fly tyers often are banded together in local clubs to share experiences and suggestions and to teach others. This leads me to make these suggestions to readers in whom this chapter strikes a spark of interest. Start the fun of fly tying just with the almost costless essentials, as the warden taught me and so many other young people to do. Read books about the hobby, and join a fly tying group. If there's one near where you live the outdoor editor of your newspaper can tell you where to find it.

CHAPTER IX

HOW TO FISH WITH SPINNING TACKLE

The spinning method of fishing calls for an open-faced, fixed-spool reel which hangs *under* the rod grip to balance the tackle comfortably for easy casting. With this type of gear the inconvenience of backlashes is eliminated; one needs little or no room for back casts, and can toss or cast small weighted lures to surprising distances. One also can fish on or near the surface or very deep down to catch fish of all sizes wherever they may be. Lures for spinning principally include live and artificial baits, small plugs, spinners, wobbling spoons and jigs. For average fresh water fishing, these should be in the ¼ to ⅜ ounce range, used with lines testing from three to six pounds—or perhaps slightly stronger if we are fishing near weeds or other obstructions.

Spinning is one of the most popular fishing methods because it is very easy to learn and because the tackle can catch almost all kinds of fish almost anywhere. This sounds so good to fishermen that many buy cheap equipment and try to use it with little or no instruction. These are mistakes they later regret. So let's learn the basic principles of how to select good tackle and how to use it properly.

Since spinning reels contain many gears and other moving parts, good ones are relatively expensive. But since one wants many years of trouble-free fishing, he should buy a quality reel with a sturdy bail pick-up, a

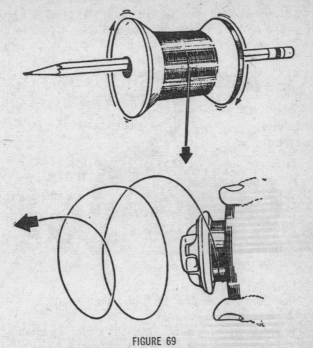

FIGURE 69
PRINCIPLES OF PLUG-CASTING AND SPINNING REELS
Line unspools from the revolving spool of a plug-casting reel. Line uncoils
from the fixed spool of a spinning reel.

drag (or brake) affording plenty of adjustment, a handy
nonreverse lock, and a reel spool which will hold at least
200 yards of line. The famous series of Eagle Claw spinning reels is one of several prominent brands which fills
these qualifications and many more. Drawing 70 illustrates one of these reels, with the names of its principal
parts. Eagle Claw spinning reels, I understand, come
with extra spools, which saves the added expense of buying them. Since we can cast lures farther with lighter
lines than with heavier ones, owning at least one extra
spool filled with line is advisable. A good choice would
be a spool of three-pound test line for making very long
casts in unobstructed water and a spool of six- or eight-

pound test line for very big fish, especially in spots where they live near weed beds, stumps and other things in the water into which fish could tangle and could break loose.

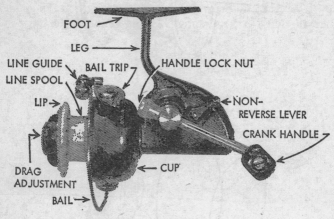

FIGURE 70
NAMES OF PRINCIPAL PARTS OF A SPINNING REEL

We also must have a rod especially made for spinning. For sturdiness and economy it should be of tubular glass. It should have graduated action all the way from tip to butt and should have little or no wobble (or "quiver") at the tip. It should have large and sturdy guides properly graduated from butt to tip and (for the average tackle we are discussing) should be about seven feet long. Two-section rods are excellent when transportation is not a problem. When the rod must be carried on pack trips, hikes and similar excursions, the four-section Eagle Claw Trailmaster is an ideal choice because, in its case, it is less than 24 inches long.

Spinning lines are relatively cheap, but they vary considerably in color, diameter and stiffness. One of the best ones (as this book is written) is a new line called "Blond" and is recommended because it is unusually strong per diameter; is of an almost invisible color, and has an ideal degree of limpness or stiffness. Such a line costs little or no more than the average, but it assures long and trouble-free casting with least danger of losing fish because of breakage.

It is very important to keep the line tight on the spool at all times. After casting, regaining line under proper

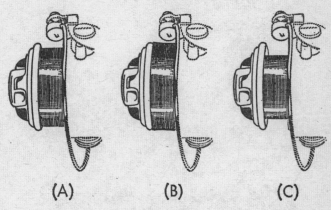

(A)   (B)   (C)

FIGURE 71
PROPERLY AND IMPROPERLY FILLED REEL SPOOLS
(a) Properly filled—to lip only
(b) Overfilled (c) Underfilled

tension is a habit very easy to learn. If you don't learn this, your next cast may result in a snarl. To avoid occasional snarls, check the line on the spool before going fishing. If it looks loose, hook the lure to something and walk backward until all the loose line is off the spool. Then walk forward, reeling under proper tension as you go. In fishing, a cautious cast reeled back in smoothly should wind loose line back onto the spool properly.

Another error commonly made is to put too much or too little line on the reel. Too little line cuts down casting distance. Too much line will result in too many coils leaving the reel together, thus resulting in snarls. The spool should be filled to the lip only, as drawing 71 shows.

Let's assemble the tackle and make a few practice

casts. Put on a lure which is heavy enough to depress the rod tip slightly (but not too much so) when the lure is reeled in to a foot or so from the rod tip. Lures in the ¼ to ⅜ ounce range should be about right for the aver-

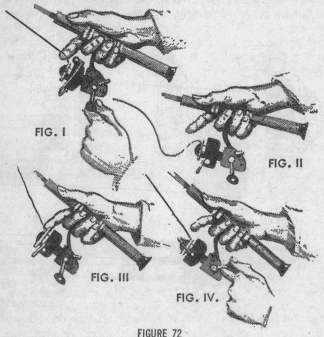

FIG. I

FIG. II

FIG. III

FIG. IV.

FIGURE 72
CASTING POSITIONS WITH A SPINNING ROD

age-strength tackle we are discussing. Remember that (in the same weights) compact streamlined lures like wobblers and jigs will cast farther than bulky or wind-resistant lures such as spinners and plugs.

The line on nearly all reels is wound on clockwise, so we'll discuss these. Most reels are made for right-handed casters; we'll describe casting with these, too. While readers who are left-handed can obtain left-handed reels, it usually is as easy and more convenient to learn the right-handed method.

Hold the rod in the right hand, as the sketches show, with two fingers in front of the reel's leg and two behind it. (Some reels are held more conveniently with one, or three, fingers in front, but these are in the minority.) Thus, when the forefinger is extended as in drawing 72(III) it can be firmly pressed against the lip of the reel spool to stop the line after a cast, or to act as an auxiliary brake. Do not transfer the rod from one hand to the other. Before making the cast, reel in until the lure is about a foot from the rod tip. This distance is needed between lure and rod tip, but more impairs accuracy. Turn the cup (either with your fingers or by turning the reel handle) until the line which passes over the line guide is nearest to the rod grip. Lift the line from the line guide with the tip of your forefinger. Avoid getting the line in the cleft of the finger joint since it can be released more accurately when it is held over the fingertip only. Now, with the left hand, open the bail by pushing it forward and downward until it clicks open. (All this is very quickly done and soon becomes habitual.) You now are ready to cast.

The side cast is the easiest one unless nearby bushes or other obstructions make some other type of cast necessary, so let's use it whenever we can. Lower the rod to the right below a horizontal position. Snap it back slightly and *immediately* sweep it upward and forward until it points over the target at an angle of about 45° above horizontal. At the instant the rod points toward the target, point the forefinger toward it also. This releases the line from the forefinger and allows the lure to soar toward the target.

The forefinger is the key to accurate control of the lure, so let's forget to trip the bail for the present. Remember how important the forefinger is! It is pointing toward the target as the lure sails through the air. To slow down the lure, all that is necessary is to move the forefinger toward the reel spool. This will cause the uncoiling line to slap against it, thus slowing down the lure.

The lure can be stopped instantly by touching the lip

of the reel spool with the forefinger. The forefinger controls the line, slowing down the travel of the lure or stopping it instantly. As the lure reaches the target, bring the forefinger slowly into contact with the reel spool. If you do it right, the lure can be stopped within a few inches of where you want it to land.

The big advantage of the side cast is that, since the lure travels in a low trajectory, the line is not caught as much by the wind as in the overhead cast. An important advantage of forefinger control is in being able to stop the line accurately. Slowing down the lure as it nears the target and stopping it as it reaches the target takes all unnecessary slack from the line. Thus, if a fish strikes as the lure lands, he can be hooked instantly because you are in control of your tackle. You also can keep the lure near the surface instead of having to fumble with slack line while it sinks. In comparison, stopping the lure by turning the reel handle to close the bail is much less desirable.

After the lure strikes the water you can put the line under control of the reel by turning the reel handle counterclockwise. The first partial turn snaps the bail closed and thus engages the line by taking it away from control of the forefinger. By delaying this, the lure can be allowed to sink as deep as desired.

Now the retrieve of the lure begins. The speed by which the reel handle is turned brings in the lure as fast or as slowly as the angler wishes. By working the rod tip, the angler can give the lure any type of motion that he desires.

The overhead cast is made in the same way except that the rod is held pointing upward. The overhead cast gives greater accuracy but has the disadvantage of a high trajectory, which puts a good deal of "belly" in the line. This is especially disadvantageous on windy days.

A cast from the left can be made by crossing the forearm across the body below the chin, pointing the rod downward, and casting forward. This is handy in making short casts when there are bushes or other obstructions to the right and above.

Let's stress again how important forefinger control is in managing the line and the lure. If the lure does not travel in exactly the right direction it is because the forefinger releases the line an instant too soon or too late. A little practice will fix that. In fishing the current of a stream the lure can be allowed to sink downstream after making the cast merely by allowing the forefinger to let a few additional coils of line slip by it. Don't bother to close the bail until you are ready to do so. That's all there is to casting and to controlling the lure—except for a little practice.

Casting with spinning tackle is leisurely casting, so don't make unnecessary work of it. One does not need to use his arm—only his wrist. To prove this, hold your elbow at your side and don't move either it or your forearm. Cast by wrist motion only. Then, if you want to compare this easy method to the too-often-seen "beating a horse" technique, try both to prove that the wrist method gets as good or better results than being overly energetic. Remember, it's the rod that does most of the work!

Many a big fish has broken off because the brake (or drag adjustment) on the reel was set too tight. To test the brake adjustment, hook the lure onto something and walk backward with the nonreverse lever engaged on the reel. It then is easy to decide if the brake should be tightened or loosened. A fairly light setting is good insurance because the spinning fisherman has two added brakes he can use temporarily. One is to press the forefinger of the rod hand against the lip of the revolving reel spool. Another is to cup the reel hand under the reel and to press against the revolving spool with thumb and forefinger. Both methods can be used at the same time, but avoid pressing too tightly because this could lock the spool and cause the fish to break loose.

An important "don't" in spinning is to avoid reeling when a fish is taking out line or when line can't be recovered because the brake is not tight enough. This accomplishes nothing except to put a twist in the line. If the reel's brake is set properly, let the fish run unless there is reason to stop him. If line must be regained and the reel cannot recover it by turning the reel handle, use one or both of the auxiliary brakes mentioned above while raising the rod to an upright position. Then reel in while the rod is being lowered. This "pumping" action can be repeated as often as desired. If the brake is set properly, avoid fooling with it when a fish is on. You may set it too tightly just when he wants to run. The result can be a snapped line and a lost fish.

In the drawing showing parts of a spinning reel, the nonreverse lever is indicated. This lever varies in appearance on various reels but usually is located in about the same place. When it is engaged, the reel can't backwind. It should not be engaged (except when trolling or still fishing) until a fish is hooked. Then it can be snapped on so the reel hand can be removed from the reel handle unless reeling is necessary.

To put a line on a spinning reel spool, assemble the rod and reel and run the line through the tip top and guides to the reel spool (with the bail of the reel open). Tie the end of the line with a Perfection Loop knot, make a noose with it, and put the noose over the spool so that when the line is pulled in a clockwise direction the loop will not slip (because it is being pulled back on itself). Set the reel's brake fairly tight and have someone hold the line spool on a pencil or something similar so the line spool will revolve when line is being taken off it. (This is because, in transferring line to the reel spool, it must be put on without twisting it.) Provide a means of tension so the line will wind on quite tightly and reel the line off the line spool onto the reel spool by turning the reel handle.

The line can be kept from uncoiling when the reel isn't being used by tying a knot in a wide rubber band to make a "tab" in it. Put the band over the line and remove the band by pulling the tab. (A rubber band without a tab knotted into it is difficult to remove.)

Even the best spinning lines, when left on the reel for a time, become set in coils which make casting difficult. Remember that the easy remedy is to hook the lure to something and to walk backward until the castable length of line is off the reel. Then, by locking the reel spool and giving the line a steady pull, the line will stretch enough to remove all coils and kinks. This also tests the line for weak spots.

Some fishermen think they should use beaded snaps, snap swivels and other linkages between lure and line. These should be used only when necessary, and they should be as inconspicuous as possible because they help to label the lure as a "fake" to fish.

When a lure has an eye neither turned up nor turned down (a "straight" eye), the Improved Clinch knot is the best one to use to tie the lure to the monofilament line. Nearly all spinning lures are so equipped. A few lures, such as wobbling spoons, sometimes only have a small hole in them for attachment to the line. In this case a snap-swivel should be attached—preferably one that is not shiny and that is as small as possible. Other similar lures are sold with a split ring through the hole. This can be attached directly to the line, as above, unless the fisherman expects to change lures often. In that case a dull-colored snap or snap swivel should be more convenient.

Since spinning lines are relatively light, "horsing" in a good fish often results in losing him. It's more fun to play them on a tight line anyway. Sharp hooks are the primary secret in hooking and holding fish, so careful anglers always keep hooks sharp and replace bent or rusted ones. Since many lures come with inferior hooks, it is well to check them to be sure they won't bend or break too easily and also to be sure the barbs are needle sharp. Many fishermen replace single hooks on lures with the reverse-bend Eagle Claw types because they know that this design "hooks and holds" better than ordinary types. Many fishermen also replace treble hooks with single hooks because the single type hooks and holds equally as well but is easier to release from a fish and also is less inclined to become tangled in the net.

Everyone gets "hung up" occasionally by the lure's catching on something underwater. Jerking the rod usually does no good. The best method of freeing the hook from an obstruction is to go in the opposite direction and then to pull on the line. If the hook still doesn't pull free, lock the reel spool on a tight line and travel backward with the rod pointing toward the hook. A strong pull usually frees the lure.

To join two lengths of line together, or to mend a broken line, use the Blood knot described in Chapter V. If the knot is tied about two feet above the lure, and a dropper six inches or more long is left on it, a fly can be attached to the dropper. This gives the effect of the fly's being chased by the lure and often results in fish being taken on one or the other—sometimes on both!

It often is said that, with spinning tackle, one can learn in a few minutes to cast well enough to go out and catch fish. While this is true, the various types of casts should be practiced until forefinger control lands the lure close to the target every time. It is amazing how easy accurate casting becomes, how much fun it is to practice it, and how thrilling it is to handle fish on this sporty, light tackle.

CHAPTER X

SPIN CASTING AND PLUG CASTING

After World War II two new fishing methods joined the familiar ones of fly fishing and plug casting (or "bait casting," as it sometimes is called). First came spinning, closely followed by what is called "spin casting." If spin casting isn't the most popular of all four methods, it surely is close to being so. This is because spin casting is a compromise between spinning and plug casting. We don't get the long casts with very light lures obtainable with spinning gear, but many people think the tackle is easier to operate. Since the reel has a fixed spool (similar to spinning) we don't get the bothersome backlashes most of us suffer from in plug casting. One can use the same heavier lures usually used in plug casting, with similarly strong lines, and can cast about as far as the plug caster can—but without the backlash nuisance.

SPIN CASTING

In the spin-casting reel, the monofilament line "spins" off a fixed (or nonrevolving) reel spool but, instead of coiling out unimpeded from an open spool, it has to travel out over the lip of the spool and down and out through a small hole (called a "line guide") in the center of the conical hood that covers the reel. While this type of design therefore requires somewhat heavier lures and stronger lines for long casts, the line is easier to control because its looseness on the reel doesn't result in the snarls beginners sometimes get in spinning or the back-lashes so common in plug casting.

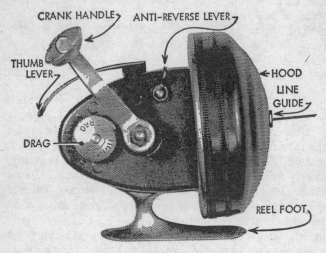

FIGURE 73
NAMES OF PARTS OF A SPIN-CASTING REEL

Spin-casting reels are available in many designs, usually quite low priced and usually with the monofilament line prespooled on them. Lines vary in strength from about six to about twelve pounds and are used with lures weighing between ½ ounce and ¾ ounce. Lighter lures require lighter lines to cast them properly, and these lighter lines can become fouled in the reel's mechanism. Slightly heavier lures can be used if they don't overtax the rod. Spin-casting tackle usually is considered to be the easiest and most nearly foolproof for the beginner who wants to enjoy general fresh water (or light salt water) fishing under varied conditions with the many types of live and artificial lures falling into its weight range.

The many designs of spin-casting reels available fall

into two general classes: the type that fits on top of the rod (which usually is used on a plug-casting rod) and the type that fits under the rod grip (which usually is used on a spinning rod). Because of this, it is well to buy both rod and reel at the same time to be sure they fit together. Which type one buys is a matter of choice, so both types should be examined and discussed. The Eagle Claw reel shown in drawing 73 fits on top of a plug-casting rod where the release lever is very convenient for thumb

FIGURE 74
CASTING WITH SPIN-CASTING GEAR

operation. Since releasing and stopping the lure is done by thumb operation, this type is very popular.

Casting with spin-casting gear is simple to learn. Reel in the lure to within a few inches of the rod tip and quickly depress the thumb lever or release lever (a button on some reels) with your thumb to prevent line from leaving the spool until you want it to. Stand sideways to the target with the rod in the right hand and with feet slightly apart. Raise the rod to a 45° angle above the horizontal. Line up the target with the rod and the right eye. Raise the rod to the vertical (but not beyond it) and *immediately* start the forward part of the cast with an accelerating "snap." At the instant the rod is back to the 45° angle, raise your thumb to release the thumb lever, thus allowing the lure to pull line off the reel. A little practice will shoot the lure in a low trajectory straight toward the target. To stop the lure over the target, merely press down on the thumb lever again. You can attain casting accuracy with very little practice.

Regaining line merely is a matter of reeling while whipping the rod, if desirable, to give added action to the lure. After making the cast the tackle should be transferred to the left hand and the reel should be cradled in the left palm to make reeling easy. Practice will suggest the most comfortable stance, and various types of casts can be tried as we have described in the instructions for spinning. As in spinning, the brake (or drag) should be adjusted to suit the strength of line being used and the fishing conditions. The position of the drag mechanism varies on different reels. All this information usually is given in the instructions which come with the reel. Also, as we learned in spinning, try to develop easy, effortless casting by letting the flexing power of the rod do the work.

Several typical casting lures are shown in Chapter VII. Since choices in lures vary widely in different areas, depending on the local types of fishing, the season of the year and other factors, it is advisable to consult experienced local anglers to learn the lures preferred in the region where one is doing his fishing. Most tackle dealers also will provide reliable advice, but some clerks don't know and there also are some who might unload on innocent beginners undesirable lures which can't be sold to anyone else.

For a generally useful collection to start with, a few wobbling lures of the "Goldfish," "Silver Minnow," "Flatfish" and "Dardevle" varieties plus a few spinners of the "Shyster" and "C. P. Swing" types will catch most game fish most times of the year. In bass regions we should add a few surface popping plugs, floating-diving plugs and deep-running ones. Don't forget the new types such as the Burke soft plastic plugs, the shiny-finish "Rebel" types and a set of plastic worms. These are killers almost anywhere. The next chapter explains how some of these lures can be made at home.

PLUG CASTING (BAIT CASTING)

Plug casting or bait casting (both names are used, but the former is more suitable today) is the angling art of casting live bait or artificial weighted lures with a *revolving spool* reel. In the hands of beginners this type of reel

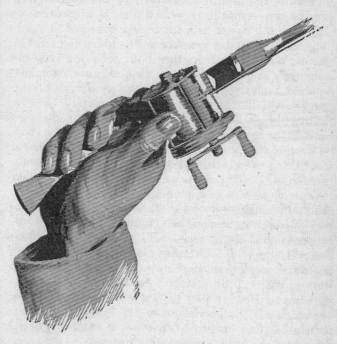

FIGURE 75
CASTING WITH A PLUG-CASTING OUTFIT

frequently overruns. That is, the energy of the cast, unless properly controlled, makes the spool revolve faster than the line goes out—so the reel spool overruns the line and causes snarls, or backlashes. These "birds' nests" can become so entangled that many fishermen have given up, thrown the outfit into the lake and adopted another method. Persistence in practice and proper instruction in "thumbing" the reel to prevent overrunning cuts down the number of backlashes, but I have noticed that even the experts get them occasionally.

Illustration 75 shows a plug-casting reel held properly in the hand with the thumb against the reel spool so the thumb can rest against the revolving spool with varying degrees of pressure to prevent the spool from overrunning and also to act as a brake when necessary. Some plug-casting reels are equipped with anti-backlash mechanisms. While these help, they don't solve the problem completely. Some plug-casting reels also are equipped with mechanical drags, or brakes, but auxiliary braking pressure with the thumb usually also is necessary.

Then there's the matter of having to spool the line back on the reel smoothly and tightly. This usually must be done manually also. All this adds up to the opinion that other methods than plug casting should be recommended for beginners. On the other hand, if the reader lives in an area where plug casting is popular, if he can find an instructor who will teach him, and if he has the patience to unsnarl his backlashes and to learn proper control of the reel—then, perhaps, this method deserves attention. Such areas usually are favorite bass and pike regions where the water is scattered with stumps, snags, pads and grasses. In such waters the shorter and sturdier plug-casting rod and the ten- to twenty-pound test braided nylon line which goes with it helps to free snagged plugs and to control hooked fish among the obstacles where they live.

Since plug casting should be only of minor interest to beginners, we'll explain it very briefly. Readers who want to know more about it should consult the very complete and authoritative information in Al McClane's *Standard Fishing Encyclopedia*, which contains twelve pages of excellent instruction on the subject.

With the tackle assembled and the lure between one and three inches from the rod tip, hold the rod in the right hand so the thumb is comfortably against the reel spool and the forefinger is hooked around the hook extending under the rod grip. Rotate the wrist so the reel handle faces upward.

For an overhead cast, extend the rod (held as above) pointing just above the target. Using more wrist motion than forearm motion, quickly raise the rod to a vertical position. The weight of the lure will flex the rod backward. Utilizing this flexing, *immediately* snap the wrist forward until the rod is pointing toward the target about halfway between vertical and horizontal. At this point, ease up on thumb pressure to allow the lure to pull line from the reel. As the lure reaches the target, gradually increase thumb pressure to slow down the revolving reel spool so it won't overrun. More thumb pressure stops the lure over the target.

To retrieve the lure, transfer the tackle to the left hand and cradle the reel in the left palm so thumb and forefinger are against the forward part of the rod grip. Reel in with the right hand, at the same time jerking the rod tip as much as necessary to give proper action to the lure. The thumb is placed on the line to provide enough tension to spool the line back on the reel evenly. If a fish takes the lure, the rod quickly can be returned to casting position in the right hand so the thumb can be used as a brake against the run of the fish. Casts from the side and underhand can be made in ways similar to those used in spinning and spin fishing.

Tackle used in plug casting is classed as ultra-light, light, medium and heavy. Ultra-light calls for weights of lures as used in spinning and, for these, the author thinks that spinning tackle is to be preferred. The light outfit uses the heavier lures used in spinning. The heavy outfit is popular for salt water use or, in fresh water, for whoppers such as muskies, pike and Pacific salmon. This leaves the medium outfit, which generally is most popular for fresh water use. This calls for lines testing from ten to twenty pounds. Select one of the lighter tests unless you are fishing for the big ones in snag-filled waters.

Lures weighing from ⅝ to ¾ ounces are correct for this tackle. Rod lengths vary from 4½ feet to 6½ feet, the longer lengths usually being preferred unless one is fishing where there are overhanging branches.

CHAPTER XI

HOW TO MAKE SPINNING
AND CASTING LURES

When I was a youngster my collection of spinning and casting lures was as small as the number of coins in my pocket. Luckily I found an older friend who was a good fisherman as well as being a man who liked to make things. One day we were fishing a river in western Massachusetts when the electric power people closed the dam and reduced the water below it to merely a trickle. While climbing around the wet rocks looking for a place deep enough to fish, we found many lures that had been caught on moss and sticks on the bottom during high water.

"Never mind fishing," my friend said to me. "Let's collect as many of these lures as we can."

"Most of 'em are busted or rusty," I objected.

"Take them anyway," he said. "There are parts we can save and use to make new ones. I'll show you how tonight."

So we each found a large can someone thoughtlessly had discarded and we filled them to overflowing with fishing lures of every possible design and condition.

That night we washed the whole mess in the sink and dried them. We used wire-cutting pliers to cut apart the wired lures and we separated all the parts—metal and glass beads, spinner blades, reclaimable sinkers, split rings, clevises, spinners, snaps, swivels and other things. We removed the split rings from the wobbling spoons,

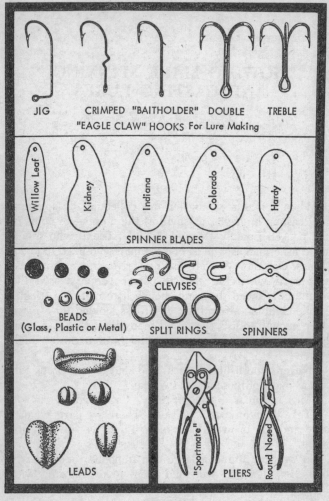

FIGURE 76
PARTS AND TOOLS FOR LURE MAKING

thus separating them from their hooks, and discarded the hooks.

"No sense in saving old hooks," he advised. "Always use new, sharp ones. The people who use rusty, bent or dull hooks are the people who lose too many fish."

The wobbling spoon blades were easy to polish with the kind of wire soap pads used in the kitchen. The enamel on some was chipped, but this did no harm. The badly scarred ones could be repainted later. New or reclaimed split rings and new Eagle Claw hooks were put on to make the spoons serviceable and attractive again. When that part of the job was done we had enough wobblers to last for several seasons.

"Now for rewiring the spinners," my friend said. "Here are coils of number 9 and number 10 stainless steel fishing leader wire I bought at a store that sells salt water tackle. Here are some red glass beads from a necklace nobody wanted, so I cut it apart. And here's a small pair of round-nosed pliers for bending loops in the wire. Cut off six or eight inches."

To show his methods we can follow the drawings on these pages. Drawing 77 shows how to make a simple spinner. Since glass beads are used, the weight at the rear is needed for casting. If brass beads were used the weight wouldn't be needed, and about seven beads could be strung on, graduated in size, with the biggest ones in the middle. Any type of spinner blade of appropriate size should work well. The forward loop is made as shown in drawing 78. This forward loop also can be made as a rear loop, but remember to thread on the hook before bending the turns of wire around the shank. The forward bead, against which the clevis (attached to the spinner) rotates, should be very small and smooth so the spinner will rotate freely. Small-diameter tubing, small egg sinkers, glass, metal or plastic beads, and even split shot can be used on the body. Things to remember are that the body should have a reasonable amount of shine or glitter and that it should be heavy enough to cast properly. Spinning lures weighing about a quarter of an ounce are excellent for average casting. Before applying the treble

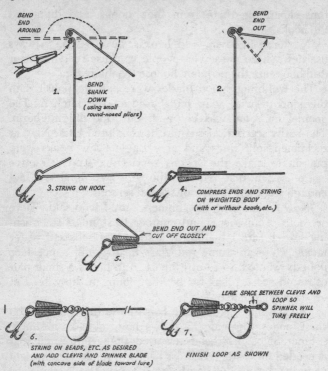

BEND
END
AROUND

BEND
SHANK
DOWN
(using small
round-nosed pliers)

1.

BEND
END
OUT

2.

3. STRING ON HOOK

4. COMPRESS ENDS AND STRING
ON WEIGHTED BODY
(with or without beads, etc.)

BEND END OUT AND
CUT OFF CLOSELY

5.

6.
STRING ON BEADS, ETC. AS DESIRED
AND ADD CLEVIS AND SPINNER BLADE
(with concave side of blade toward lure)

LEAVE SPACE BETWEEN CLEVIS AND
LOOP SO
SPINNER WILL
TURN FREELY

7.

FINISH LOOP AS SHOWN

FIGURE 77
HOW TO ATTACH HOOK FOR SLIDING OR FIXED BODY

hook it can be dressed with bucktail of one or more colors. Chapter VIII explains how to do it. Lay a very small bunch of hair between each of the shanks of the treble hook, so three bunches are used in all, tied in one at a time. White, yellow and red (or combinations of them) are good colors.

This is all we need to know to make a large assortment of spinners in many sizes, designs and color combinations. Some typical ones are shown in drawing 82. With only a little practice, anyone can bend and loop stainless steel leader wire properly—and of course stringing on the various parts of the body is easy, and fun!

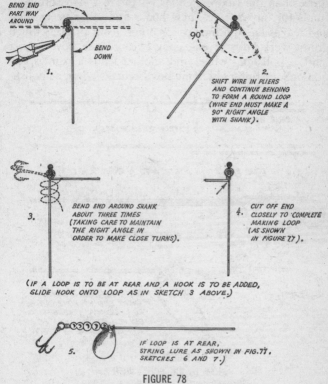

BEND END PART WAY AROUND

BEND DOWN

1.

90°

2.

SHIFT WIRE IN PLIERS
AND CONTINUE BENDING
TO FORM A ROUND LOOP
(WIRE END MUST MAKE A
90° RIGHT ANGLE
WITH SHANK).

3.

BEND END AROUND SHANK
ABOUT THREE TIMES
(TAKING CARE TO MAINTAIN
THE RIGHT ANGLE IN
ORDER TO MAKE CLOSE TURNS).

4.

CUT OFF END
CLOSELY TO COMPLETE
MAKING LOOP
(AS SHOWN
IN FIGURE 77).

(IF A LOOP IS TO BE AT REAR AND A HOOK IS TO BE ADDED,
SLIDE HOOK ONTO LOOP AS IN SKETCH 3 ABOVE.)

5.

IF LOOP IS AT REAR,
STRING LURE AS SHOWN IN FIG. 77,
SKETCHES 6 AND 7.)

FIGURE 78
HOW TO MAKE A FORWARD OR REAR LOOP

Those who can't scrounge enough spare parts can buy them cheaply. If tackle stores don't carry them, you'll find them listed in mail-order catalogs such as Herter's, Inc. of Waseca, Minnesota.

Some of the lures we have bought occasionally become damaged. Why not rebuild them instead of throwing them away? Several Scout groups make valuable projects of this. They leave contribution boxes at sportsmen's clubs so members can drop damaged or unwanted lures into them for repair and reuse. The boys enjoy rainy evenings doing repair work, and take a reward of a few lures; then the troop auctions off the rest. This provides funds for buying wire, new hooks and other necessities, and leaves enough money for other Scout projects. Such group work adds to efficiency because one boy's father lends a polishing wheel and another lends a paint spray gun or something else. One boy becomes adept at polish-

1   BEND WIRE DOUBLE
(AROUND SMALL NAIL OR NEEDLE NOSED PLIERS)

2   BEND LOOP END DOWN (NEARLY TO A RIGHT ANGLE)

3   SLIDE LOOP OVER HOOK, PUTTING ENDS THROUGH EYE

4

CONTINUE WITH RIGGING
(SHORT END OF WIRE CAN BE
RUN PART WAY THROUGH RIGGING;
CAN BE LOOPED, OR CAN BE BENT
AND CUT OFF AS IN FIG. 77)

FIGURE 79
HOW TO RIG HOOKS WITH
TURNED-UP OR TURNED-DOWN EYES

ing, another at enameling, and so forth. The work is a pleasure, and the pleasure makes a profit!

Hooks on most spinners are linked without being rigidly wired to the lure, as we have described. All such hooks should be straight-eyed (with the eye turned neither up nor down). This attachment is used mainly because fish have less chance to shake loose a nonrigid lure. But sometimes we want a rigid attachment, or we want to use a hook with a turned-up or turned-down eye. The method of wiring them is shown in drawing 79. After wiring, the body can be built as has been described.

To attach a treble hook rigidly, the wire is bent double and applied as shown in drawing 80. You'll need two pairs of pliers to pull these rigid attachments tight.

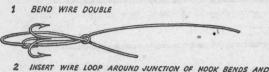

1 BEND WIRE DOUBLE

2 INSERT WIRE LOOP AROUND JUNCTION OF HOOK BENDS AND THROUGH EYE, WITH SHANK AND END GOING THROUGH EYE IN OPPOSITE DIRECTIONS. PULL TIGHT (USING TWO PAIRS OF PLIERS).

3 BEND SHORT END OF WIRE AROUND SHANK ABOUT THREE TIMES. CUT OFF SHORT END.

FIGURE 80
HOW TO WIRE TREBLE HOOKS RIGIDLY

A spinner with a snap on its end often comes in handy because we can change the hook easily, putting on singles for attaching worms and other baits, artificial flies of many types (on straight-eyed hooks), bare doubles or trebles, or these dressed with various colors of hair or feathers. This method is shown in drawing 81, and it also is a way to make a snap, if the store kind isn't handy.

Six different homemade spinners are shown in drawing 83. No. 1 is called a "turkey bone," and is especially good for catching bass. The single hook can be attached rigidly or loosely, or we can use a loose double or treble. This lure is called a turkey bone because that's what it originally was made from. Nowadays we take a four-inch piece of ¼-inch-diameter red rubber tubing—the more flexible the better. We cut the middle two inches apart on a very narrow diagonal, so each piece is three inches long, with a one-inch tube and two inches of tapered tail. Push an egg sinker or a metal bead of suitable size into the tube end so it is concealed and so it can be threaded onto the wire as shown. Add a smooth glass bead for the spinner and clevis to revolve against and string them on. Make the wire loop at the head of the lure, and it is finished. Other colors of rubber can be used, such as white or yellow, but I have had better luck with the red.

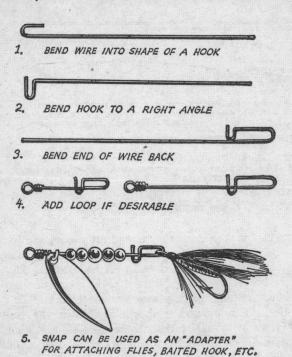

1. BEND WIRE INTO SHAPE OF A HOOK

2. BEND HOOK TO A RIGHT ANGLE

3. BEND END OF WIRE BACK

4. ADD LOOP IF DESIRABLE

5. SNAP CAN BE USED AS AN "ADAPTER" FOR ATTACHING FLIES, BAITED HOOK, ETC.

FIGURE 81
HOW TO MAKE A SNAP

No. 2 is a spinner with several (five, six or seven) brass beads strung on the body to give the lure shine and weight. No. 3 has a brass (or other metal) tapered body with a smooth red bead for the propeller to revolve against. In making this one, allow room on the wire for the propeller to revolve freely. No. 4 has a treble hook decorated with very fine pieces of red rubber bands. These pieces (about 1½ inches long) can be strung through the eye of the hook and tied down in the middle

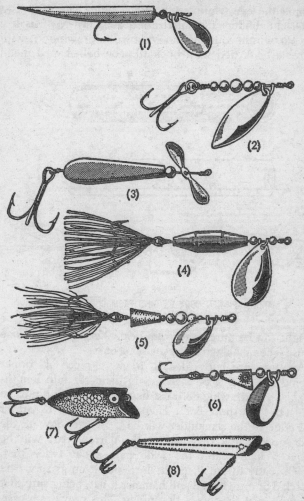

FIGURE 82
HOMEMADE SPINNERS AND PLUGS

behind the eye while being pulled tight. The body is a tapered cylinder of painted cast lead. Lure No. 5 is like the one whose construction is shown in drawing 77, with a treble hook tied with bucktail. The bell-shaped metal

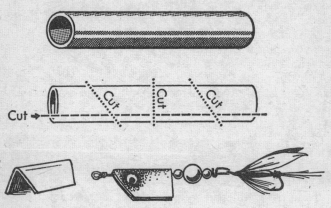

FIGURE 83

MAKING SPINNER BODY WEIGHTS FROM COPPER TUBING

weight can be purchased from dealers and is a good one to use when making the turkey bone lure.

Another lure body idea is to saw a piece of copper tubing which is ¼ or ⅜ inches in diameter into lengths as shown in drawing 83. First hammer the tubing into an oval (but not quite flat). Then use a hacksaw to cut off one edge so the remainder will be U shaped. Saw off the first section at a diagonal so the narrow part will be about ⅜ inches and the wide part about twice that. When ready to put it on the lure, put it on as shown in sketch 6 of drawing 82 and hammer it flat, being sure that the wire is at the top of the tubing. This provides a casting weight as well as a streamlined body which can be enameled in any color (such as red, white or yellow), to which painted eyes could be added. A tiny drop of enamel on the end of a matchstick is enough for the eye and (when dry) a pupil can be put in the eye with a tiny drop of enamel of another color applied with the end of a toothpick. Glass beads and a spinner blade complete the lure.

Drawing 76 also shows a flat heart-shaped lead. Very small ones of this type (usually obtainable from tackle dealers and used as keels) can be bent over the wire to form similar weighted bodies. They should be tapped in place tightly with a hammer. Plumbers use sheet lead which can be cut and applied similarly.

Since spinner and wobbler blades are so easy to obtain, making our own seems too much trouble to be worthwhile, but let's touch on it briefly. A spinner or wobbler shape can be traced on any flat piece of metal, such as a can cut open and flattened out. Metal snips or a hacksaw will cut it to shape and the edges can be smoothed with a file. Holes can be punched or drilled for the split rings or clevises. The metal can be pounded into dish shape against a piece of wood by using the rounded end of a ballpeen hammer.

The first wobbler undoubtedly was evolved from the bowl of a teaspoon, with handle sawed off and with holes bored at both ends for the split ring, hook and snap swivel. Since that day the wobbler, or wobbling spoon, in all sizes, colors and designs, has been of great importance to fishermen. The spoon handle also can be used in the same way and can be bent slightly to adjust it to provide the right wiggle. Handles of most spoons are too big for lures for fresh water fish, except possibly for pike and a few other big ones, but they make excellent salt water lures. The treble hook should be dressed with hair such as polar bear or bucktail.

Plugs are fun to make, and simple ones are quite easy. Cut them from hardwood dowels between ½ and ¾ inches in diameter, such as the handles of discarded small brooms, mops or garden tools. An expedition to the town dump should produce enough dowels to last indefinitely—especially the shaped ones found in certain kinds of furniture. These, when cut in appropriate places, provide shaped bodies which save work.

To turn these pieces of wood into plug bodies, cut them to size and shape them with jackknife, file and sandpaper. Discarded plugs will furnish screw eyes and disc washers but, if these are not enough, new ones can be bought cheaply from supply houses. Note that these screw eyes are very thin, so they won't split the wood. The kind found in the family workbench usually is too thick. Before inserting them, drill a very small-diameter hole to guide in the screw eye properly and to avoid splitting the wood.

Designs for plugs can be copied from favorites in tackle boxes. The shaping of the head and the place where the screw eye is inserted are important to proper action of the plug. If the head is cut flat and cupped, you'll have a popping plug. If it is cut at an angle, it will be a floating-diving plug like the one shown in sketch No. 7 in drawing 82. Metal lips and other accessories to make more complicated types are available from tackle dealers or tackle mail-order houses.

Before inserting the screw eyes and crimping the hooks to them, the plugs should be painted. First, dip them in a priming paint. When dry, add any colors desired. If masking tape is put around the plug, the front color and the rear color can be separated sharply. A piece of screening laid over part of the plug allows the paint spray gun to apply paint with a fish scale effect. Sinking plugs are made by drilling two or three holes under the keel and putting lead in them. These then are sealed with plastic wood.

Interesting plugs like the one shown in sketch No. 8, drawing 82, can be made from discarded ink pens. Remove the rear end of the pen and saw it off to the right length and angle. Drill a small hole for the forward hook (if you want one) or (with plastic pens) burn it through with a hot nail. Insert the wiring as has been described for making spinners. Then fill the cavity with plastic wood, plaster of Paris or lead. Plastic wood, of course, makes a more buoyant plug than the other two materials.

Let's conclude this lure-making lesson by quickly describing how to make jigs, because small ones are as useful in fresh water fishing as they are in salt water. The hook used is the type of Eagle Claw jig hook shown in drawing 76. We can make molds of plaster of Paris or other materials but, since this is a bit complicated, let's remember that tackle supply houses sell them cheaply and also provide detailed instructions. The hooks are inserted in the mold and the mold is closed. Liquid lead or white metal is poured into the cavities to fill them. The mold can be opened almost immediately to remove the jigs. These then can be filed or whittled to remove excess metal. Hair tails are put on as described in Chapter VIII. Then the heads of the jigs can be dipped in paint and hung up to dry. If we want them, decorations such as painted eyes can be applied as we have described.

From this we see that anyone can make simple lures very cheaply and easily, or that he can progress into more complicated ones as a hobby. Those which require several kinds of paint and a few tools, such as plugs and jigs, often are handled as group projects. In this way cost and work are divided. Some of the lures made by group projects can be sold to pay for materials needed to make more. This is an economical way to fill our tackle boxes —and perhaps even to make a profit!

CHAPTER XII

LET'S ENJOY FISHING SAFELY!

Fishing is one of the safest of sports, and probably it would be the most safe if everybody always used as much common sense as they should. Carelessness and lack of knowledge sometimes cause mishaps; we hope this chapter will help you learn ways to prevent them. Over the years the author has had several fishing mishaps, such as a broken leg, a hook in his hide, and several dunkings of one sort or another. All were due to carelessness, and none was very much fun. So let's read this chapter carefully to see what we can do about it.

The path to the river was well worn and seemed safe. If I hadn't stepped on that green tuft of grass just off the path, it would have been. But the tuft concealed a small and very deep hole. As one of my legs went into it the other one snapped, and the cast I had to wear for several months was a constant reminder that I should have watched my step. Luckily I had two companions I could use for crutches on the short trip back to the car and the hospital. If I hadn't, probably the alternative would have been to lie quietly and call out at intervals until someone came along to help.

The point to be made is that this wouldn't have happened if I had been watching my path to be sure I didn't step on doubtful ground. Most fishing accidents of that sort happen in foolish leaps from rock to rock, where one could slip and do serious damage. Wet, mossy rocks are slipperier than one might think, and dry ones aren't always very safe to land on, either. Felt-soled waders or boots help a great deal, but don't depend too much on them for sure footing.

I enjoy wading fast streams. There's a trick to crossing swift currents when you're nearly waist deep in them. Walk crossways to the current to block its pressure as little as possible. Put one foot ahead of the other slowly and be sure it is firmly planted before taking another step. If things get a bit ticklish, don't panic, because you can't make a run for the shore. Stand still and figure things out. Don't be afraid to call for help if necessary.

In such waters, fish with someone else so a companion will be nearby if needed. A stout pole to help prop yourself against the current is handy, but remember to find one and take it with you before getting in too deep. An inflatable life vest or belt is very sensible to wear on many rivers. In case of trouble, just trigger the gas cartridge to inflate it.

Be careful when wading unfamiliar waters, and don't take chances even on familiar ones. When wading down a fast current, be sure you know how you're going to get out. Once I fished down a riffle in the middle of a stream which flowed into a deep pool. On reaching the point of the riffle, with deep, fast water all around, I found I couldn't back up. The only alternative then was to tighten the belt around my waders, slip into the deep water and make like a boat. I don't recommend trying to swim when wearing waders!

After doing a few foolish things like that, one learns to be careful. It's smarter to learn to be careful beforehand, so you won't do foolish things like that!

Fishing from a boat presents an entirely different set of circumstances. A boat is extremely safe when used sensibly. It can be quite the contrary when it isn't. Boating people respect others who are sensible and considerate. They have no use for the other kind. The other kind includes people who overload the boat.

In stepping into a small boat, step in the middle, as near the center as possible. Keep low and use the sides of the boat to help you. Get set before the next person comes aboard. Never jump, even if it seems safe. You could break your leg (or your neck) that way, too! Before boarding, have all your gear on the dock within easy reach, because long reaches from boat to dock can cause trouble. Trouble not only could spoil your own day, or even your whole vacation. It could spoil it for the others, too.

Sensible people think life preservers (which include ring buoys, buoyant vests and buoyant cushions) always should be taken along no matter how good the weather is—one for every person aboard. In fact, the Coast Guard and most camps and resorts insist upon this. Check them in before leaving and be sure everyone knows how to use them. If anybody can't swim, be sure he *wears* one.

Having a man overboard usually isn't serious if the others use common sense. Falling out of a boat almost always is the result of one foolish action or another. In changing places in a small boat (which usually shouldn't be done anyway) only one person should move at a time. He first states his intention to move, and then he lets the others help him. Standing up may be safe in some boats and under some conditions, but not always. Only one person should stand at a time, in any case. He should stand near the middle, avoiding shifting his feet as much as possible. In fly fishing, the person who is standing has an advantage, but standing and moving should be discouraged except under ideal circumstances.

When one of your pals does fall out of the boat, what do you do? If rowing, extend an oar or throw him a length of line and lead him around to the stern. Help him aboard over the transom. If in an outboard, throw the stern away from the swimmer and shift to neutral. Throw him a cushion or ring buoy. When you're sure he is clear of the propeller, circle around quickly and approach him headed into the wind, or waves. Shut off the motor when beside him and, using a paddle or a length of line, lead him around to the stern and help him aboard. In case of serious trouble, such as with a person who has gone underwater, try to reach him with a paddle. Avoid diving for him unless you're an expert swimmer, and unless you can anchor the boat. If canoeing, help the man to the stern and let him hold on while you paddle to shore.

Squalls can blow up on lakes and even ponds, changing their surfaces quickly from a placid calm to very rough water. When away from shore on big water it's common sense to keep an eye on the sky—especially the western sky, because that's where most of the weather comes from. Dark, low clouds usually predict a storm and the storm usually brings winds and high waves. At the first sign of bad weather, expert boatmen head for home or, at least, toward shore. If you don't want to go in, spend periods of questionable weather fishing along the shoreline so it will be easy to scoot for safety if necessary. The lee shore (the side the wind comes from) will be calmer.

When caught out in rough weather, head into, or quartering into, the waves, because waves hitting the boat broadside may turn it over or, at least, make it very rough going. Waves coming from behind could slop over the transom and swamp the boat. Have all hands put on life-preserver equipment, or at least have it within easy reach. Try to travel at a speed which keeps as little water as possible from coming aboard. Figure your course to get into quiet water at the earliest moment, even if it's not where you want to go. Safely ashore, you know the wind will quiet down before long—so relax until the return trip can be made safely.

It may seem unnecessary to stress these points. If you think so, you may remember having read about capsized boats being found after storms with no one aboard. The people who were aboard are spending a wet hereafter in Davy Jones' locker because they didn't pay attention to the sensible rules of boating safety.

And what should you do if the boat does tip over? Everyone should stay with the boat, being sure that the people who can't swim well are being taken care of. Sometimes the boat can be righted and some of the water can be sloshed out of it by rocking it. Then one person can get aboard over the stern and try to bail it out. Usually, however, it's best for everyone to hang onto the boat and wait for help. Even if help isn't quick in coming, this is the safest course. While you're waiting, wind and waves probably will drift the boat to shallow water.

And now, what about safety with fishhooks? I've watched strangers swing treble-hooked lures around at the tips of casting rods as if they were trying to imitate the Lone Ranger lassoing a steer! I've seen lures land in people's hats, in their jackets and occasionally in their hides. This isn't any fun for anybody, and we should be very careful to avoid it.

The first time I ever saw a hook in a man's hide was on a lake in the north country when I was fishing with Ross McKenny. I walked down to the dock and watched Ross casually but carefully sharpening his jackknife. (Ross was an expert guide and famous with the fly rod —so this can happen to anybody!)

"Fishing no good?" I inquired.

"Don't know," he answered, testing the knife blade with his finger. "I wish you'd help me get this fly out of my shoulder. It's where I can't reach it."

The fly was firmly imbedded, and we were fifty miles from a doctor.

As I helped with pliers and knife, Ross chatted calmly.

"Damn fool thing for me to do," he lamented. "I should know enough not to cast on the windy side with this breeze coming down the lake. The wind caught the line on a sloppy cast and dug this little streamer right into me. Anyway, I'm the biggest one I've caught all day! I'm a new kind of a fish. You can call me a 'chump.'"

These things happen, very suddenly, even to the best of us. But they almost always happen through carelessness—and here's how we can avoid them:

In fly fishing, especially on breezy or windy days, always cast on the side of you toward which the wind is blowing. Thus, if a gust of wind blows the line out of control, the fly will blow away from you. If people are nearby, be sure they are on the safe side—the side on which the wind can't blow the fly near them. This is especially important when two or more people are fishing from a boat. Watch your back cast and be sure it is safe.

When people are casting close together, regardless of the tackle being used, only one should cast at a time. Let the other fellow make the first cast. While he is retrieving his lure it's your turn. Use the overhead cast rather than the side cast. Watch your back cast here, too. Good fishermen work together as a team, casting safely, one at a time. They watch their lures and lines to be sure the lures can't come dangerously close to anybody, regardless of conditions. Thus, we rarely ever hear of anybody being harmed by fishhooks.

Sometimes sportsmen are so far away from medical attention that a hook in the hide requires first aid on the spot. Since advice about removing embedded hooks should be given by a doctor of medicine, a highly experienced one was asked to provide it for this book.

"A deeply embedded hook should not be removed on the spot unless it will be several days before the patient can reach a surgeon. The average fishhook in the skin is not much different than a large sliver. Calm down your unfortunate buddy—and yourself, too. All will be well.

"Whether the hook is to be removed later by a doctor, or by someone now, first do these things:

"Have the patient lie down—*flat*. Insist on this! If not, he may faint or vomit and make the situation miserable for himself and for you. Don't let him watch you work. Make him turn his head away.

"Now, clear the area. Remove or cut off clothing. Cut off line or leader. Separate the hook from the lure, with cutting pliers, for instance. All that remains above the skin now is the hook shank. Below the skin is the barb and part of the bend of the hook. If one hook of a treble is imbedded, cut off the other two so that the treble is converted into a single hook.

"If the person can be taken to a doctor within a reasonable time, immobilize the hook by putting a Band-aid, some tape or something similar over it, first perhaps pouring a small amount of Merthiolate or other antiseptic around the wound. Take the person to a doctor as soon as possible.

"If it seems necessary to remove the hook on the spot, inform the patient that what is to follow will be uncomfortable, with some tugging of the hook shank. However, the average person can endure this, as well as an occasional sharp twinge, if he is told in advance to expect it.

"Most fishhooks can be removed by gripping the hook with a pair of fishermen's pliers and pushing the hook backward, away from the barb, and then gently manipulating it back along the path of penetration. In a case where the barb is still imbedded and cannot be backed out, a sharp, thin-bladed knife can be inserted along the side of the shank of the hook to release the barb from the tissue so it will back out.

"Finally, cleanse the area. Soap and water are fine. Apply a clean dressing, such as a handkerchief. Do not exercise the injured area if at all possible, since pumping action from motion could spread infection. Get medical attention from a physician or hospital as soon as possible to be sure that the hook removal has been handled properly."

All well-equipped fishermen carry pliers—usually of the Sportmate type. These have strong gripping jaws as well as a cutter which will cut any usual hook suitable for fresh water use.

Fishing safely is like driving a car and doing many other things where we have to handle our own affairs and, at the same time, watch out for what the other person might do. Fishermen—real fishermen, that is—are noted for being courteous, helpful and thoughtful of the welfare of others. That's about all anyone needs to enjoy fishing safely!

CHAPTER XIII

AND NOW, LET'S COOK THEM!

One of my most enjoyable days out fishing began on a June morning when Jim Simon and I roamed a beaver meadow in the shadow of the majestic snow-capped Grand Teton mountains near Jackson Hole, Wyoming. The brook, rainbow and cutthroat trout were big, and rushed from hiding places under the banks of the deep and winding stream to grab tiny artificial nymphs cast to them on long and very fine leaders. We hooked and landed many that morning, but kept only one for lunch.

Jim had a small fire going in the protection of a large rock on a gravel bar. He had produced a flattened roll of super-strength aluminum foil from his pocket and was crimping a large doubled piece to make a cooking pot. On the rock were several strips of bacon wrapped in foil. He also had brought small vials of salt and pepper and a lemon.

"Looks like a fat lunch you've got there," I said. "What do I get, the bacon or the lemon?"

"Boy!" he exclaimed, "you're goin' to eat high off the hog today. I found a hatful of morel mushrooms in the woods. While I clean and wash and split them, suppose you go along the bank and bring back a great big bunch of dandelion greens. Pick the young plants that have buds but no blossoms."

When I returned with the greens, the foil pot he had made was half full of mushrooms. We added the cleaned

160

greens, a little water, some salt and pepper and the juice of half the lemon. We set this on the coals and the liquid soon began to simmer. While it simmered, we stirred the greens and mushrooms with a clean twig to be sure they all cooked evenly. Meanwhile, Jim cleaned and filleted

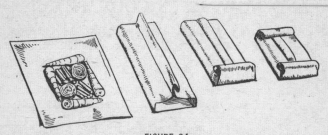

FIGURE 84
THE "DRUGSTORE FOLD" PACKAGES FOOD TIGHTLY FOR
COOKING IN THE COALS OF A FIRE
(Lay food in center of foil. Gather opposite ends and fold over together at least twice. Do the same with both sides to make a tight package.)

the trout and laid each of the two big fillets on a sheet of the foil. He put a slice of bacon on each and salted and peppered them.

"I see you know how to make the 'drug-store fold,'" I said as he wrapped the packages to go on the fire. "That's a good, tight way to seal them so no juices will leak out."

"Yes, and we'll wrap each of them double," he said. "That way a small puncture does less damage, and the packages are stronger and easier to handle. On these coals, not over ten minutes on each side should be long enough to cook them. Fish isn't half as good when it's overcooked."

While he watched the food I cut two small Y-shaped branches and pointed the ends so they could be used as forks. When I returned, the packages were off the fire and had been opened on the rock.

"We had a little juice in each package," he said, "so I tilted it into the greens. Should be good! Now we'll share the pot of greens and mushrooms, but you'll have half the trout all to yourself."

We squeezed a little of the remaining half of the lemon over the fillets and enjoyed one of the most delicious lunches I've ever had. Everything except the food which nature had provided could be carried easily in a pocket.

"What would you have done if we hadn't caught a trout?" I asked.

"I always carry insurance," Jim said. "I've got a hunk of elk salami in my pocket. We could have added slices of it to the greens and it would have been quite good."

Smart fishermen usually carry little outdoor cooking essentials such as these in their pockets. Several squares of heavy-duty foil can be folded together, handkerchief-like, and carried with negligible bulk and weight. The sort of plastic vials some small fishing lures come in are excellent for salt and pepper or other condiments. A larger jar can carry instant coffee, mixed with sugar and powdered cream if desired. Cups, plates, pots and cooking packages are easily fashioned from foil. So if you think you might want to cook outdoors, why not carry your kitchen equipment with you?

Cooking fish—and other parts of the meal—outdoors is quite simple. A secret of fish cookery is not to overcook them. When the flesh flakes off the bones, they are done —and this takes less time than one might think. Another secret is to use hardwoods for your fire, because evergreens are pitchy and inclined to smoke. Make the smallest fire that will do the job, and let it burn down to coals. Large fires are unnecessary and hard to work over, and they might get out of hand. Small ones are less liable to singe the cook or burn the food.

Since part of the fun of fishing is to cook what we've caught, the following easy recipes should be worth remembering. We'll start with three more very simple outdoor methods and will include several others which can be done either outdoors or at home.

FISH ON A STICK

This is a way to broil small fish—something like the way we used to toast marshmallows on a green stick

FIGURE 85
HOW TO BROIL FISH ON A FORKED STICK

when we were kids. The fish is cleaned, and scaled if necessary. The head can be left on, but cooking seems a bit easier if it's cut off. All we need is to cut a fairly sturdy green branch about two feet long, with a fork at the end. The tips of the fork are whittled to sharp points. Impale both points inside the front part of the body cavity, being sure the fish is on securely. Toast it over moderate heat about five minutes to a side. When the thick part of the flesh flakes off the bones, it is done. If the fire is not too hot the skin will be crisped and dark brown. Add salt and pepper, if you have any, and eat the fish right off the stick!

PLANKED FISH

This is a good way to broil large fish when we have no broiler or similar equipment. A clean heavy board will do, but half a short log is better if it will stand up securely on both ends. As drawing 86 shows, the head and tail of the fish are cut off and the fish is slit in two, but the two sides should not be separated. Nail the fillets to the log or board, or wire them on securely. Stand the log (or prop the board) in the heat of the fire. To test the heat, put your hand in front of the fish. If you can hold it there comfortably for a few seconds, but not longer, the heat should be about right. Cooking should take about 15 minutes, but the log or board should be turned once during that time to broil all sides of the fish evenly. It helps to baste nonfatty fish (like trout or bass) with bacon fat during the cooking. Test the flesh and stop cooking as soon as it flakes easily and is nicely golden brown. Add condiments and eat it off the wood.

BAKED TROUT ON A ROCK

Heat a flat, dry rock in the campfire until it is very hot. While the rock is heating, clean the fish, remove its head

FIGURE 86
PLANKED FISH

and cut it open without separating the two sides. When the rock is hot enough, poke it out of the fire and clean the top by whisking it with an evergreen bough or a bunch of green grass. Lay the fish on the rock, skin side down. Add salt and pepper, plus a little bacon fat or butter, if you have any. Let it bake on the rock until the flesh becomes flaky and the bones can be removed easily. The skin will stick to the rock, and you can use the rock for a plate. (Rocks taken from a stream may be porous enough to hold water which could turn to steam and break the rock, so select dry ones.)

These outdoor cooking suggestions and the recipes which follow are taken from *The Outdoor Cook's Bible*, which is one of the books suggested for supplementary reading in the list at the end of this book.

FISH CHOWDER (HOME STYLE)

> 6 or 8 strips bacon, cut in small pieces
> 2 large or 3 medium-sized onions, chopped fairly fine
> 2 pounds fish fillets or pieces, cut small
> 3 large or 4 or 5 medium-sized potatoes, diced
> 1 teaspoon salt
> ½ teaspoon pepper
> 1 teaspoon dried herbs (marjoram and/or thyme, or herb blend)
> 3 cups water (or stock, if you have any)
> ½ cup cream or canned milk
> 1 can condensed cream of celery soup (or other cream soup)

Fry the bacon pieces in a skillet until crisp. Remove from fat and drain them. (Diced salt pork can be substituted.) In the fat, sauté the chopped onions until translucent but not very browned. Put the fat and onions into a fairly large kettle or Dutch oven and add the fish, potatoes, salt, pepper, herbs and water or stock. Let this simmer until potatoes and fish are cooked. Then add the cream or milk and the cream soup. Let this simmer awhile longer before serving, but don't let it come to a boil. Taste it to see if it needs any more salt or condiments.

Serve the chowder in big bowls, with crackers. Sprinkle some of the crisp bacon pieces on top of the liquid in each bowl. Remember that this chowder tastes even better after it has been allowed to stand in a cool place (such as a refrigerator) overnight.

Some chowder addicts chop a green pepper and sauté this with the onion. I have heard of foreigners (usually people from New York State) who make chowder "Coney Island" style. This consists of adding about ¼ cup of tomato catsup and 2 cans of tomato sauce instead of the milk and cream soup. In New England we shoot people for doing things like that.

FISH CHOWDER (CAMP STYLE)

This one will have to be played by ear as far as the ingredients go.

In a Dutch oven or kettle place a thin layer of diced salt pork or bacon. On top of this place a goodly layer of boned fish, with skin removed. Then add a layer of thinly sliced potatoes and a layer of thinly sliced onions. On top of this put a thin layer of soda crackers. Dot this with butter and add salt and pepper to taste. Repeat the process until you have put in enough to feed all hands. Add enough water to fill the pot about halfway up. Cover the pot and let it simmer until the contents are cooked. The liquid should be allowed to cook away, so that the bottom layers of bacon and fish are browned. Then add cream (or diluted canned milk or, preferably, diluted cream soup) to cover. Heat again until it is steaming hot, but don't let it boil.

This chowder, of course, can be made in the coals of a campfire, if a Dutch oven is used.

FRIED POND FISH

> 4 or more small pan-dressed pond fish, such as white
>   bass, perch, bluegills or crappie
> 2 cups pancake mix
> 1 egg, beaten
> 1 small bottle ginger ale or 7-Up
> 1 cup vegetable oil, bacon fat or other shortening
>   Salt and pepper to taste

Combine one cup of the pancake mix with the egg and enough of the pop to make a thin batter. Dip the fish in the other cup of dry pancake mix and let them dry for 15 minutes or so. Then sprinkle the fish with salt and pepper and dip them in the batter. Fry until golden brown. The batter will puff up as the fish cook. (In all fat frying, the fat should be very hot but not smoking.

Test it with a small piece of bread dropped into the fat.
If the bread bubbles and browns quickly the fat should
be hot enough, but don't add more fish unless the ones
you have put in are bubbling briskly.) Drain the fish on
paper toweling after frying.

FRIED FISH

Here's another good way to fry small fish or fillets:

> 6 or more small fish such as smelt, trout or fillets
> 1 cup flour
> ½ teaspoon salt
> ⅛ teaspoon pepper
> 3 tablespoons olive oil
> 3 tablespoons butter
> Juice of 1 lemon
> ¼ cup chopped parsley

Mix the flour, salt and pepper, and toss the fish or fillets in it to coat them thoroughly. Fry them slowly in
the mixture of oil and butter until golden brown. Transfer to a platter. Add the lemon juice to the fat and pour
it over the fish. Garnish with the parsley. (See note in
the recipe above about correct temperature for frying.)

FISH CAKES

> 2 cups cooked fish, shredded
> 4 medium-sized potatoes, freshly boiled and hot, put
> through a ricer or chopped very fine
> Salt and pepper to taste
> 1 small onion, minced (optional)
> ¼ teaspoon curry powder (optional)
> 3 eggs
> 1 cup dry bread or cracker crumbs
> ½ cup butter, margarine or bacon fat

Combine the fish, potatoes, onion and seasoning. Stir
in the eggs (stirring as little as possible). Shape the mixture into cakes and dip them in the crumbs. Fry in the
butter or fat until brown.

The fat should be fairly hot and bubbling, as for any
other kind of fat frying. If a food grinder is available, the
fish, potatoes and onion can be put through it, rather
than preparing them separately.

If salt codfish is used, first rinse it in hot water and, preferably, soak it in water overnight to remove the salt. Omit salt in seasoning. Canned fish may also be used. In this case, omit salt. Traditionally, in New England, fish cakes are served with tomato sauce or catsup.

BROILED WHOLE FISH

> 1 or more fish, dressed (and scaled, if necessary)
> Salt and pepper to taste
> 1 or more onion slices for each fish
> 2 bacon or salt pork slices for each fish

Dry the cleaned fish and add salt and pepper to taste. Put onion slices inside the body cavity. Place a slice of bacon or salt pork on each side of the fish, and clamp them in a wire broiler. Broil over the coals for 10 minutes or more (depending on size of fish) until flesh flakes off bones when tested for doneness with a fork.

BOILED FISH

> About 2 pounds of fish fillets (salmon, striped bass, trout, fresh-water bass, etc.)
> 1 cup finely chopped parsley
> 1 garlic clove, finely chopped
> 1 small onion, finely chopped
> Salt and pepper to taste

Cut the fish into slices about 1 inch thick and put them in a frying pan. Barely cover them with water. Add remaining ingredients. Cover the pan and allow the fish to simmer for 20 minutes or so, until cooked. Remove fish to a platter and serve with melted butter or the Creole Sauce described in the last recipe in this chapter.

Fish cooked this way is excellent when served either hot or cold. This makes a jellied fish dish when thoroughly chilled.

If we lack certain flavorings, we can get along very well by improvising with something else. Outdoor cooks should carry an herb bag or a variety of herbs and other condiments. The addition of these various flavorings can transform an ordinary dish into a chef's masterpiece. For example, if you don't care for garlic and onion flavors, leave them out of the above recipe and substitute 2 tablespoons of vinegar or lemon juice.

BAKED FISH

    1 large fish, 4 pounds or more
    2 bay leaves
    2 slices bacon
    2 slices onion

Line a pan with aluminum foil and put the bay leaves, bacon and onion on the foil so that the fish will be on top of them. (This helps to flavor the fish and prevents sticking.) Lay the fish (cleaned and wiped dry) on the bay leaves, bacon and onion, adding seasoning on the fish, if desired. Bake at 400° or 425° in a preheated oven, not over 12 minutes per pound. Baste the fish occasionally with whatever juice is in the pan. Test it to be sure it is not being overcooked. This is an easy recipe, and is one of the author's favorites. The sauce in the next recipe goes very well with it.

CREOLE SAUCE

    1½ cups canned tomatoes
    1 green pepper, seeded and sliced very thin
    1 medium-sized onion, sliced very thin
    1½ cups mushrooms, sliced very thin
    1 tablespoon flour
    1 teaspoon butter (or margarine or oil)
    1 beef bouillon cube
    1 cup hot water

Combine the first four ingredients; bring to a boil and simmer about 10 minutes. Melt the butter separately, and blend in the flour over low heat until smooth. Dissolve the bouillon cube in a little water and stir it into the blended flour. Then add the first four ingredients and cook slowly for 2 or 3 minutes. Add a little more of the water if the sauce is too thick. This makes about 2 cups of Creole Sauce.

Put the fish on an ovenproof platter and pour the sauce

over it. Sprinkle on about 1½ cups of fresh buttered bread crumbs, if handy. Put the platter under the broiler for a minute or two, until the sauce is properly browned. (The sauce can be made up in advance, kept in the refrigerator and heated when needed.)

BRING 'EM HOME FIT TO EAT!

Good recipes and expert cooks don't add up to tasty fish dishes if fishermen spoil their catch before they get it home. The finest fish ever caught may be as tasteless as damp cardboard if he's been allowed to slosh around in the water in the bottom of a boat for part of a day—or if he's been left lying in the sun, especially when we've forgotten to clean him.

If you hanker for flavorful fish dishes that really are delicious, give the cook a fair chance. Keep your catch cool and dry; clean the fish as soon as possible, and get them to the refrigerator, the freezer or the skillet as quickly as you can.

This can be done even under adverse conditions. Once I wanted to bring home a pair of beautiful, big brook trout caught on a wilderness lake, but the trip back to civilization would take two days and we had no refrigeration. We cleaned the fish immediately, wiped them dry, and rolled them inside and out in corn meal. Then, while still cool from the water, we wrapped them tightly in several thicknesses of newspapers. The corn meal helped to keep them dry and prevented their sticking to the paper. We kept them stored in the coolest places, and they were as tasty as freshly caught ones when served a few days later.

Nowadays we have portable refrigerators which we often take along anyway, even on wilderness trips. Plastic bags and the corn meal idea keep fish fresh in the ice boxes, and prevent them from contacting other foods. If the fish are prepared for cooking before rolling them in the meal, all that is necessary later is to pop them into a hot skillet. Many fishermen consider creels a nuisance and prefer to keep the catch in plastic bags, even when temporarily carried in the game pockets of fishing jackets.

CLEANING THEM IS EASY!

After catching them, take a break and clean the fish as soon as possible. A small, sharp sheath knife helps. My favorite has a four-inch blade with grooves on the top for scraping off scales. Hold the fish, belly up, in the palm

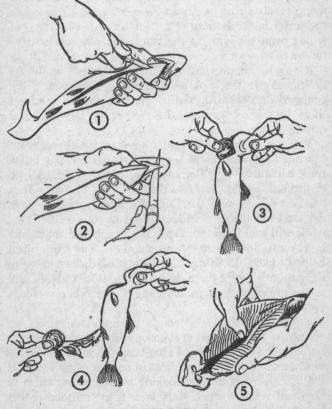

FIGURE 87
HOW TO CLEAN A FISH

of your hand, with thumb and forefinger in the gills so you'll have a good grip. Slit the skin open from vent to gills, and make a cross cut at the head to sever the lower junction of the gills from the skin. Get a good grip on the gills and pull backward, thus pulling out all the gills and the "innards." If part of any gills are left in, pull these out too, because they would hasten spoilage.

With this done, you'll see a black streak down under the backbone. Scratch this with the point of the knife to slit the membrane which covers it. Then use your thumbnail to push out all the dark material. Since this also hastens spoilage, be sure it's all removed, with any membrane remnants along with it. Scale the fish if necessary. You can postpone this until later but, if you use the corn meal treatment, it's better to do it now. Finally, wipe the fish as dry as possible, and store it where it's cool.

HOW TO FILLET FISH

If you wish to cut the meat off the bones to obtain fillets, it's not necessary to clean the fish if this is done fairly promptly. Lay the fish on a flat surface and make

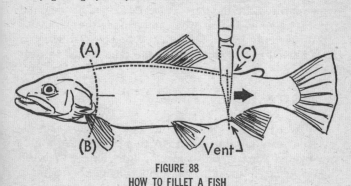

FIGURE 88
HOW TO FILLET A FISH

a cross cut just back of the gill covers from "A" to "B," as shown in drawing 88. The cut is made all the way down to the backbone at the top of the head, and you'll get most meat by sloping the knife slightly forward, just back of the bony part of the head. The depth of the cut grows less as you cut down to the neck—just deep enough to slice the flesh, but not enough to cut into the body cavity.

Next, make a deep cut from this one along the top of the back, as close to the dorsal fin as possible. Slice this down to the backbone. Now, at point "C," insert the knife with blade flat and pointing backward so you can push it through the flesh to the vent. To get all the flesh possible, let the knife follow along the backbone and slice backward until the back of the fillet is sliced free.

Your fingers now can pull the flesh near the head away from the row of spines which includes the dorsal fin. Holding the meat of the fillet upward, use the knife to slice the meat off the ribs. As the fillet is cut free, it is easy to cut along the ribs down to the belly of the fish. A few slices along the ribcage will free the fillet and, if the job has been done properly, nearly all the meat will come off with the fillet.

Do the same on the other side, and you have two fillets. All that's left is the head and tail, connected by the skeleton, with the body cavity untouched. While we sometimes remove the innards (as described above) and pop the rest into the chowder pot, usually these remains are of use only to the family cat. (You probably could have filleted two or three fish in the time it took to read this!)

HOW TO SKIN THE FILLETS

I've watched salt water charter-boat captains skin fillets; they can do it in seconds. With a sturdy, sharp, narrow-bladed knife whose blade is a little longer than the fillet is wide, it shouldn't take much longer, even for a beginner. Lay the fillet, skin side down, on a flat surface. Starting at the tail end, make a small slice along the inside of the skin to start to separate the meat from the skin. Holding this small end of free skin, lay the knife flat along the inside of the skin and push it forward with

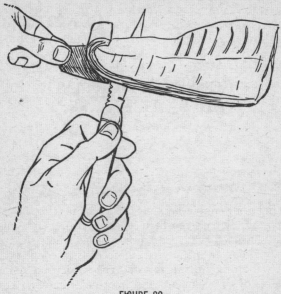

FIGURE 89
HOW TO SKIN FILLETS

a slight sawing motion. A flat cut will make the knife follow along the skin to slice the skin free with no meat left on it. (Some people use pliers to hold the end of the skin, but I've never seen experts bother with them.) A glance at drawing 89 should quickly show how this is done.

CHAPTER XIV

CONSERVATION AND
HOW IT WORKS

When our forefathers first settled in this country, nearly all of our northern coastal rivers and inland streams teemed with sport fish such as trout, shad and salmon. They swept in from the oceans in countless migratory hordes, up the forested rivers, beyond the settlements of the colonists, and into the tributary streams where they had been born. There they laid their eggs in the gravel of the cold, clear water so their kinds could be perpetuated in the abundance so lavishly planned by God for the uses of man.

In those days the streams were banked and shaded by cool, damp forests. Countless gallons of water were stored in the spreading root systems of each tree, to be released gradually, cold, clean and clear, in times of need when snows were gone and drought threatened.

Where towns sprang from the wilderness the trees were cut to build homes and factories, and to provide fields and gardens. They were cut without planning or replacement because planning and replacement then were not needed. But when too many were cut they laid bare the watersheds, thus parching the soil. When heavy rains came, the remaining trees in many places had insufficient root systems to hold back the water. So it tore down in floods, eroding the soil, silting the food-bearing stream bottoms and even changing the courses of the streams themselves.

With too many trees gone, man built dams to hold back the floods he had caused, and to provide power for manufacturing and for his cities. The dams also held back the fish, preventing their migratory journeys to their source waters. The fish grew fewer and fewer. And with the shading trees gone, the waters in many places became so warm the fish were forced to leave them or die.

In early days man also dumped into these streams the sewage from his homes and the refuse from his factories. This then was so little that it seemed harmless. But as man grew in numbers the pollution of our waters increased. Year by year it kept on increasing until most of the streams and rivers became open sewers in which fish could not live. As the factories multiplied, the quantities of filth dumped into our waters also multiplied—chemicals, dyes, sludge and everything else that was unwanted and that would float away. They still are doing so. So in most places people no longer can drink the water, or even use it for swimming, boating and other forms of recreation. The countless migrating hordes of sport fish long have been gone, and in too many of our rivers even trash fish cannot remain.

Gradually, more and more people became alarmed at this wanton and needless destruction of our priceless national heritage. They dug the word "conservation" out of the dictionary and tried to explain to factory owners and city politicians what it meant. They reminded these people that conservation means "the wise uses of our resources"—our soil, our minerals, our forests, our waters and our wildlife—and that they had better start paying attention to it because these resources did not belong only to them. But the thoughtless, selfish and greedy ones among the factory owners and politicians paid little or no heed because conservation didn't pay dividends and it didn't get votes.

So, to prevent further destruction and to try to remedy the colossal damage which had been done, conservation-minded people formed into groups. The Izaak Walton League, Trout Unlimited and the Federation of Fly

Fishermen are among them, ably supported by youth groups such as the Boy Scouts, Girl Scouts, Camp Fire Girls, 4-H Clubs and many others. Groups such as these began to teach the meaning of conservation, and their memberships multiplied. Farsighted factory owners began to realize that lack of attention to conservation was very bad business, and that their stockholders didn't like it. Politicians who had turned deaf ears to the demands for city sewage-treatment plants and other conservation projects began to realize that this shortsightedness was costing them votes, and that they therefore had better do something about it. Mayors, governors and even the President of the United States began to listen to the vital messages these conservation-minded groups are sending.

So, at long last, things are being accomplished. But meanwhile our population continues to grow. As it grows, wilderness areas become fewer and fewer, while there are more and more fishermen to enjoy our lakes and streams. Fortunately, growing numbers of people are becoming conservation-minded. The fish hog who yanks in too many too often no longer is looked upon with tolerance. He is regarded as a thief. Anglers may keep an occasional trophy, or bring home a few fish for dinner, but they are learning that there no longer are enough for everybody, and that it is wiser to fish more for fun and less for meat. People who discard refuse thoughtlessly rarely are ignored when they are caught at it. They are liable to hear very unfavorable remarks very audibly made about them, including the suggestion that they should pick the stuff up and take it to a proper place for disposal. We are beginning to realize that the great out-of-doors is part of our home, that we should preserve it while we enjoy it, and that we should make it clean.

This is the duty and the privilege of everybody, and it will take the efforts of everybody to repair the damage which has been done. If a letter to a congressman, a senator, a governor, or even to the President seems in order, don't think that, because you are only an individual, it won't get attention. The attention and action such letters get is surprising—if there are enough of them.

There is another side to this conservation picture and, fortunately, it is much more encouraging. States have Departments of Natural Resources formed to aid conservation. A unit of these is the Department of Fisheries and Game, or whatever a particular state calls it. This department has the responsibility of maintaining and improving our fish and game for the enjoyment of all people. Their hatcheries raise fish for stocking streams and lakes, into which the fish are planted at suitable times of year. Their wardens roam our woods and waters to protect and conserve our wildlife for the benefit of all. They do not act as policemen unless necessary. They are the friends of sportsmen, and are there to help. "Where's the best bass lake around here?" "What fly or lure should I use?" "Is it all right to build a fire to cook lunch?" "I'm having trouble with my tackle. Will you help me a bit?" Questions like these are asked of wardens constantly. They usually know the answers and are pleased to provide them.

Wardens (or "game protectors," as many of them more correctly are called) are dedicated men who work very hard for the small pay they get. If the trip is long and hard, and if the weather is at its worst, they'll be doing their jobs anyway, and they'll be doing them night and day. If someone gets hurt in the woods, they'll help him. If he becomes lost, they'll find him. If a family of beavers dams a road, they'll fix it, and they'll probably move the little animals somewhere else. If something is killing the fish in a stream, it's their business to find out why, and to report what action should be taken. They perform countless other services too. I have many friends among wardens, and every one I ever met was a very fine person.

The salaries of these people largely come from revenues obtained from selling fishing and hunting licenses. Such funds also build and stock hatcheries which provide many of the fish we catch. They pay to protect stream banks from erosion, and to provide such things as deflectors and small dams in streams so more and bigger fish can live in them. The money from licenses does a great deal more for fishermen. So buying a license is a good investment, and we always should carry one.

Sport fish (but not usually those referred to in this book as "trash fish") are protected by law in most regions. Since laws vary in various states and regions it is important to obtain the booklet on state fish and game laws from your town or city hall (or from tackle dealers) and to study it. This booklet or folder specifies the open seasons for various species, tells minimum lengths or weights of fish which may be kept, and gives bag limits and other information to which all fishermen must conform. This is because (in many areas) small fish must be returned to the water to grow up; closed seasons are necessary to permit fish to remain unmolested for spawning; catching fish where they concentrate at certain times (such as below dams) might be too easy, and thus harm fishing later; some fishing methods (such as netting, spearing, using lures with too many hooks, etc.) might spoil sport fishing, and so on.

Fishing laws are necessary to insure good fishing, even though we don't always know the reasons for some of them. Since they are made for our benefit, they should be carefully obeyed. One law that's most important isn't in the fishing regulations. It is: "If you would catch more, you must kill less."

One of the most important parts of conservation is what our old friend Smokey the Bear tries to teach—the prevention of forest fires. People unused to the woods often build fires that are too big or in the wrong places, or are careless about putting them out. Many presumably dead fires have started up again because they were built over underground roots. Even when drenched with water, fire can smolder underground in the roots of removed trees, only to break out and cause serious damage several days later. Thus, fire regulations must be obeyed. Lacking any, we should be doubly careful.

Up in Maine, where I like to go fishing, a big sign

greets arrivals into the wilderness. I have mentioned it in other books, and would like to do so again. It says, "This Is *God's Country*. Why Set It on Fire and Make It Look Like *Hell?*"

Having fun fishing is so big a subject that no book can cover it all. I hope readers will think that this one includes the essentials. From here on, one has to become more or less specialized, so the final pages list a few other books that may be of interest. I apologize because three were written by myself. They are included because I know of no others which seem to cover the subject.

As stated in the introduction, this book is made possible because the makers of Eagle Claw fishing tackle share with me the opinion that beginners (especially young people) should have a book at the lowest possible cost which teaches the elements of fishing. I hope this one does. Since the folks at Eagle Claw seem to be rather modest about providing it, I shall (without their permission) include their address in case anyone wishes to write to them about it. It is: Wright & McGill Company, 1400 Yosemite Street, Denver, Colorado 80220.

REFERENCE BOOKS

The following books are available at bookstores and/or libraries and are considered valuable for reference:

FISHING (General)

THE FRESH-WATER
FISHERMAN'S BIBLE, by Vlad Evanoff
(New York: Doubleday & Co.), $1.95.
This large-size, well-illustrated 180-page paperback describes basic fresh water fishing outfits, plus chapters on all types of fresh water fish, with suggestions for catching them.

McCLANE'S STANDARD
FISHING ENCYCLOPEDIA, by A. J. McClane
(New York: Holt, Rinehart & Winston), $19.95.
The most complete book on fish and fishing ever published; written by 141 scientists and angling experts, supervised by A. J. McClane, world-famous fishing editor of *Field & Stream*. Its 1,088 pages describe over 1,000 species of fish, angling methods, fish biology, fly tying, casting, rod making, etc. This valuable book is expensive only because it is so big.

TRICKS THAT TAKE FISH, by Harold F. Blaisdell
(New York: Henry Holt & Co.), $3.95.
299 pages of excellent ideas that do what the title says. Well illustrated by sketches and written by a reliable authority.

THE TROUT FISHERMAN'S BIBLE, by Dan Holland
(New York: Doubleday & Co.), $1.95.
A large 190-page well-illustrated paperback that describes the various species of trout, their habits, what they eat and how to imitate fish food with artificial lures; tackle, and casting with all types of fresh water equipment.

FLY FISHING

COMPLETE BOOK ON FLY FISHING, by Joe Brooks
(New York: A. S. Barnes & Co.), $4.95.
Considered by many to be the greatest fly fisherman of all time, this author explains the intricacies of fly fishing

for beginner and expert: fly choice and presentation, selection of tackle for fresh and salt water species, and suggestions for improving casting and fishing success.

FLY TYING

FISHING FLIES AND FLY TYING, by William F. Blades
(Harrisburg, Penna.: The Stackpole Co.), $8.50.

A large 320-page excellently illustrated book describing the tying of all types of wet and dry flies and nymphs, bass and salmon flies, and jigs, etc., together with the dressing formulas for hundreds of patterns. This book is especially valuable for its entomological information on imitating specific flies and nymphs with artificials.

FLY TYING, by Helen Shaw
(New York: Ronald Press Co.), $7.00.

Over 250 clear, life-size photos, with specific instructions, in this 282-page book take the fly dresser through all details of fly dressing and the uses of materials, as done by a noted professional. As a how-to-do-it book this is the very best, but it does not provide dressing formulas for specific patterns.

HOW TO TIE FLIES, by E. C. Gregg
(New York: Ronald Press Co.), $1.95.

This book contains only 84 pages, and it has been around for many years, but it still is an excellent low-cost text for the beginner.

STREAMER FLY TYING
AND FISHING, by Joseph D. Bates, Jr.
(Harrisburg, Penna.: The Stackpole Co.), $7.95.

This 368-page book is the world authority on streamer fly and bucktail patterns and their histories, providing detailed, authentic tying instructions for over 300 patterns exactly as dressed by their originators. It contains instructions on how and why to select specific patterns for all conditions, and how to fish them for all fresh and salt water game fish. Eight full-page plates show 119 of the most famous patterns in full and accurate color.

FLY TYING AND TACKLE MAKING

PROFESSIONAL FLY TYING
AND TACKLE MAKING, by George L. Herter
(Herter's, Waseca, Minnesota), $1.50.

A big 416-page book at a very low price, describing fly tying and equipment, tackle making, and how to make several other types of lures. Since this book gives a lot for a little, and contains information unavailable elsewhere, every fisherman should have it.

OUTDOOR COOKING

THE OUTDOOR COOK'S BIBLE, by Joseph D. Bates, Jr.
(New York: Doubleday & Co.), $1.95.

This is included because you should know how to cook what you catch! It is a 212-page profusely illustrated paperback describing outdoor cooking with little or no equipment, and on to more elaborate methods. This big book also provides hundreds of excellent recipes for cooking all kinds of fish and game, and how to do it. It is used widely as a manual by Scouting groups.

FREE FOR THE EATING, by Bradford Angier
(Harrisburg, Penna.: The Stackpole Co.), $4.95.

When cooking fish, either outdoors or in, it's fun to eat off the land! This authoritative 192-page book illustrates and describes over 100 varieties of edible plants, berries, roots and nuts, and tells how to identify and prepare them. You'll find many in your own back yard.

SPINNING

SPINNING FOR
FRESH WATER GAME FISH, by Joseph D. Bates, Jr.
(Boston, Mass.: Little, Brown & Co.).

This 254-page book is the most complete text on spinning with the open-faced reel. Published in 1954, it currently is out of print but available in libraries. It provides detailed instructions on tackle and tactics, and how and where to cast for all fresh water game fish under all conditions.